Gooseberry Patch Co.

Quick & Easy
Autumn

D0553478

Gooseberry Patch
2500 Farmers Dr., #110
Columbus, OH 43235

www.gooseberrypatch.com

1·800·854·6673

Copyright 2011, Gooseberry Patch 978-1-936283-36-1
Second Printing, March, 2011

All rights reserved. No part of this book may be reproduced or
utilized in any form or by any means, electronic or mechanical,
including photocopying and recording, or by any information
storage and retrieval system, without permission in writing
from the publisher. Printed in Korea.

Do you have a tried & true recipe...

tip, craft or memory that you'd like to see featured in a **Gooseberry
Patch** cookbook? Visit our website at **www.gooseberrypatch.com**
to share them with us instantly. If you'd rather jot them down by hand,
use the handy form in the front of this book and send them to...

Gooseberry Patch
Attn: Cookbook Dept.
2500 Farmers Dr., #110
Columbus, OH 43235

Don't forget to include the number of servings your recipe makes,
plus your name, address, phone number and email address.
If we select your recipe, your name will appear right along
with it...and you'll receive a **FREE** copy of the cookbook!

Table of Contents

Dedication

For those who love all the flavors of fall...and having the time to savor them too!

Appreciation

We're thankful for everyone who shared their family's tried & true recipes!

Breakfast & Brunch

Spiced Harvest Pancakes

Shelly Smith
Dana, IN

A wonderful waker-upper on a cool fall morning!

2-1/2 c. biscuit baking mix
1 c. milk
1 c. apple butter
2 T. oil

1/2 t. ground ginger
1/2 t. cinnamon
1/2 t. nutmeg
2 eggs, beaten

Stir together all ingredients until well blended. Pour about 1/4 cup of batter per pancake onto a hot griddle that has been sprayed with non-stick vegetable spray. Cook over medium heat until pancakes start to bubble; flip and cook until golden. Makes about one dozen.

Dutch Honey

Katie Cooper
Chubbuck, ID

At our house, pancakes and French toast are always served
with a pitcher of Dutch Honey! My father-in-law
handed down this simple recipe.

12-oz. can evaporated milk
1-1/2 c. corn syrup

1-1/2 c. sugar

Combine ingredients in a small saucepan over low heat. Cook and stir until sugar is dissolved. Serve warm; refrigerate any leftovers. Makes 15 servings.

Watch for old-fashioned syrup pitchers at tag sales...set out a variety of sweet toppings like flavored syrups and honey for pancakes and waffles.

Breakfast & Brunch

Scrumptious Apple Pancakes

Charlotte Smith
Tyrone, PA

*These pancakes are so yummy! I like to serve them on
a cool autumn day, along with warm apple cider.*

2 c. pancake mix
1 c. chunky applesauce

1 c. water
1/2 t. cinnamon

Preheat an electric griddle to 375 degrees or heat a stovetop griddle
over medium-high heat. Mix all ingredients in a bowl. Drop by
1/4 cupfuls onto lightly greased griddle. Cook until pancakes bubble;
flip and cook until golden. Makes about one dozen.

For an autumn brunch, serve fresh-baked muffins
and scones tumbling out of a wicker cornucopia
basket...it'll double as a buffet decoration.

Good Morning Sausage Casserole

Beth Bundy
Long Prairie, MN

*I received this hearty all-in-one breakfast recipe from an
old friend...it's become a family favorite!*

8-oz. tube refrigerated crescent
    rolls
1 lb. ground pork breakfast
    sausage, browned and
    drained

6 eggs, beaten
1/4 c. milk
salt and pepper to taste
2 c. shredded Cheddar cheese

Unroll crescent rolls into the bottom of a greased 13"x9" baking pan.
Spoon browned sausage over rolls. Beat together eggs, milk, salt and
pepper; pour over sausage. Sprinkle cheese on top. Bake, uncovered,
at 350 degrees for 25 to 30 minutes. Makes 15 servings.

Start a tailgating Saturday right...invite friends to join you for
breakfast! Keep it simple...a make-ahead breakfast casserole,
baskets of sweet rolls and a fresh fruit salad. Add mugs of
hot coffee and cocoa if it's chilly, or cold cider if the weather
turns balmy. It's all about food and friends!

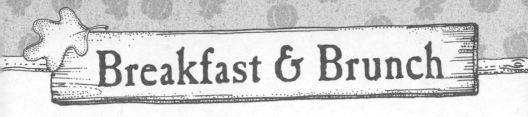
Cheesy Sausage Ring

Debra McClure
Roanoke, VA

*I love this three-ingredient breakfast recipe I discovered recently!
It's so simple to put together, and you can use different flavors of
sausage and cheese to change it up.*

2 12-oz. tubes refrigerated
  biscuits
1 lb. ground pork breakfast
  sausage, browned and
  drained

2 c. shredded Monterey Jack
  cheese

Flatten each biscuit to a 3-inch circle. Arrange 12 biscuits in the
bottom of a Bundt® pan sprayed with non-stick vegetable spray,
overlapping if necessary. Spread browned sausage evenly over biscuits
in pan. Sprinkle cheese evenly over sausage. Cover with remaining
biscuits. Bake at 375 degrees for 22 to 25 minutes, until biscuits are
golden. Turn out of pan onto a serving plate; let stand 5 minutes
before cutting. Serves 8.

Visit a nearby farmers' market for just-harvested
fruits & vegetables, eggs, baked goods, jams &
jellies...perfect for a farm-fresh breakfast!

Cranberry-Lime Cooler

Ellie Brandel
Milwaukie, OR

A refreshingly different beverage for an autumn brunch.

6-oz. can frozen limeade,
   thawed
4 c. cold water
16-oz. bottle cranberry juice
   cocktail

1/4 c. orange drink mix
ice cubes
Garnish: fresh mint sprigs

Prepare limeade with water in a large pitcher. Stir in cranberry juice and orange drink mix. Pour over ice cubes in tall mugs or glasses. Garnish each with a sprig of mint. Makes 8 servings.

Serve beverages in old-fashioned Mason jars. Setting the jars inside wire drink carriers makes it easy to tote them from kitchen to harvest table.

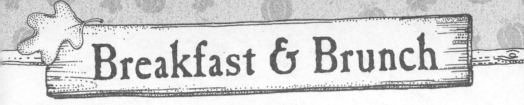

Breakfast & Brunch

Angela's Special Smoothie

Kim Burrell
Manitoba, Canada

I've been making this recipe for years...my little daughter Angela loves fruit smoothies! Don't be tempted to use vanilla-flavored soy milk, as it will make the smoothie too sweet.

1 c. frozen mixed berries
1 c. plain soy milk

1/2 c. bananas, sliced
2 t. honey

Place all ingredients in a blender. Process on high setting until smooth, thick and well blended, about 30 seconds. Serves 2.

For an on-the-go breakfast, spread cream cheese or peanut butter and your favorite dried, chopped fruit on a bagel. So easy...and tasty!

Apple Cider Syrup

Ben Gothard
Jemison, AL

*Treat yourself...this warm syrup is yummy drizzled over pancakes,
waffles and homemade biscuits!*

1/2 c. sugar
1/2 c. light brown sugar, packed
2 T. cornstarch
1/4 t. cinnamon

1/4 t. nutmeg
2 c. apple cider
1 T. lemon juice
1/4 c. butter, softened

In a saucepan, mix together sugars, cornstarch and spices. Pour in
apple cider and lemon juice, mixing well. Cook over medium heat until
thickened and boiling, stirring constantly. Boil and stir for one minute;
remove from heat. Stir in butter before serving. Makes 14 servings.

My brother-in-law invites us to glean his garden at the end of
summer. My grandkids and I dress in our garden gear of jeans,
long-sleeved shirts, "puddle jumper" garden boots, pulled-up
socks and sun hats for our annual vegetable rummage. The
delights and treasures we find are endless! We can always count
on more than enough tomatoes, peppers and onions to make our
favorite sauce. Later, on the snowiest, coldest day of winter, we
go to my freezer and pull out our summer bounty. All the
sunshine, laughs and giggles from that end-of-summer day
come back as we sit down and say grace together.

-Kathie Poritz, Burlington, WI

Upside-Down Apple Coffee Cake

*Amy Hunt
Traphill, NC*

*This recipe was shared with me by a childhood friend who's still
a very special part of my life. It's delicious and so easy to make.*

1-1/2 c. apples, peeled, cored,
    chopped and divided
12.4-oz. tube refrigerated
    cinnamon rolls, separated

1/2 c. pecan pieces
2 T. butter, melted
1/3 c. brown sugar, packed
2 T. corn syrup

Spread one cup of apples in a 9" glass pie plate sprayed with non-stick
vegetable spray. Cut cinnamon rolls into quarters, setting aside icing
from tube. Place rolls in a large bowl; add remaining apples and
pecans. In a small bowl, combine remaining ingredients; mix well and
pour over rolls. Toss gently to combine. Spoon mixture over apples in
pan. Bake, uncovered, at 350 degrees for 25 to 35 minutes, until rolls
are deep golden. Cool for 5 minutes; invert onto a serving platter.
Remove lid from icing and microwave for 10 to 15 seconds. Drizzle
icing over warm coffee cake. Make 8 servings.

Autumn is time for apple fun. Pick your own apples in an
orchard, watch cider being pressed at a cider mill or go to
a small-town apple butter stirring. Ask about different
varieties of apples...you're sure to find a new favorite!

Leather Bread & Tomato Gravy

Courtney Chapman
Moravia, IA

My grandmother has made this simple dish as long as I can remember. While she cooks, Grandmother tells me stories of her own mom & dad making many of the same recipes. Her daddy often made this Leather Bread. Grandmother wrote down many of her recipes for me, so I'll always be able to make her dishes too, and remember the times we shared cooking together.

1/4 c. oil, divided
1-1/2 c. self-rising flour
1 c. milk
28-oz. can whole tomatoes,
    chopped

2 T. sugar
1/4 c. shortening
salt to taste

Spray a cast-iron skillet with non-stick vegetable spray; put 2 tablespoons oil in skillet. Mix together flour, remaining oil and milk; pour batter over oil in skillet. Bake at 375 degrees for 35 minutes. Remove from oven. Cool bread in skillet for 5 to 10 minutes; invert onto a plate. Combine remaining ingredients in skillet. Cover and bring to a boil over medium-high heat. Reduce heat and cook for several minutes, until thickened to desired consistency. To serve, slice bread and cover with tomato gravy. Serves 6.

A sweet keepsake for a family brunch. Copy one of Grandma's tried & true recipes onto a festive card, then punch a hole in the corner and tie the card to a rolled napkin with a length of ribbon.

Breakfast & Brunch

Simmered Eggs in Tomatoes

Janis Parr
Ontario, Canada

Don't let the simplicity of this recipe fool you...it is delicious!

2 T. olive oil
1 c. stewed tomatoes, cut up
1/2 c. onion, chopped

4 eggs
salt and pepper to taste
buttered toast

Heat oil in a skillet over low heat. Place tomatoes and onion in oil;
cook for 5 minutes. Drop eggs into skillet, one at a time; add salt and
pepper. Cover and simmer until eggs are cooked through as desired.
Serve hot on buttered toast. Makes 2 servings.

Leftover potatoes make scrumptious home fries! In a heavy
skillet, heat one to 2 tablespoons oil until sizzling. Add 3 cups
cubed cooked potatoes and 1/2 cup chopped onion. Cook for
5 minutes. Turn potatoes over and season with salt, pepper and
paprika. Cook another 5 to 10 minutes, to desired crispness.

Lisa's Easy Maple French Toast

Lisa Staib
Broomfield, CO

French toast with the syrup cooked right in! I use a pizza cutter to quickly cut the toast into triangles for my younger children. Top with jelly, sliced fruit or more syrup if you like.

1 T. butter
4 eggs
1/3 c. maple syrup

4 slices bread
1/4 c. brown sugar, packed
1/8 t. cinnamon

Melt butter in a large skillet over medium-low heat. In a shallow bowl, beat eggs and syrup together with a fork. Slowly dip each slice of bread into egg mixture on both sides. Fry in skillet until golden; flip gently and cook other side until golden. Sprinkle with sugar and cinnamon. Serves 4.

How beautiful on harvest-slopes
To see the sunshine lie;
Or on the paler reaped fields
Where yellow shocks stand high!

-Mary Howitt

Freezer French Toast

Gloria Warren
Ontario, Canada

A friend gave this recipe to me. I love French toast, but don't have time to prepare it on those busy mornings. This pops from freezer to toaster!

5 eggs, beaten
1-1/4 c. milk
1-1/2 T. sugar

1/2 t. salt
16 slices white bread
Garnish: butter, maple syrup

In a shallow bowl, combine eggs, milk, sugar and salt; mix well. Dip bread slices on both sides; place on baking sheets coated with non-stick vegetable spray. Bake at 500 degrees for about 5 minutes, until golden on bottom. Turn over; bake for 2 more minutes. Allow to cool, then freeze toast slices in a single layer. Once frozen, about 2 hours, package toast slices in individual plastic freezer bags. To serve, remove toast slices from bag. Heat in a toaster or toaster oven; garnish as desired. Makes 16 servings.

Tickle the kids at breakfast with Jack-o'-Lantern oranges. Slice the tops off navel oranges and scoop out the pulp with a spoon. Draw on silly or spooky faces with food coloring markers. Spoon in fruit salad and serve...clever!

Spinach & Onion Quiches

Kelly Gray
Weston, WV

I first made this recipe one day when some relatives came to visit, a whole week early! I whipped it up in a panic and prayed...it was a hit! These quiches are now requested by all my family members and church friends. Try them with leeks & sausage or bacon & red pepper...delicious. These quiches keep well in the fridge and taste even better the next day.

2 9-inch pie crusts
1 onion, diced
1 T. oil
8-oz. pkg. sliced mushrooms
1 T. dried oregano
1 t. dried thyme
1-1/2 t. salt

1 t. pepper
10-oz. pkg. frozen spinach,
   thawed and squeezed dry
8 eggs, beaten
3/4 c. light cream
2 c. shredded mild Cheddar
   cheese

Place pie crusts in two, 9" pie plates. Bake at 350 degrees for 8 minutes, until golden. While crusts are baking, sauté onion in oil in a skillet over medium heat for about 8 minutes. Add mushrooms; continue sautéing for 6 additional minutes. Stir in seasonings; cool slightly and transfer to a large bowl. Add remaining ingredients; mix thoroughly. Divide mixture evenly between pie crusts. Bake at 350 degrees for 25 minutes, or until bubbly and set. Makes 2 quiches; each serves 6.

Make a quick, savory crumb crust for a quiche. Spread 2-1/2 tablespoons softened butter in a pie plate, then firmly press 2-1/2 cups seasoned dry bread crumbs or cracker crumbs into the butter. Freeze until firm, pour in filling and bake as directed.

Breakfast & Brunch

3-Cheese & Onion Omelet

Tiffanie Ansel
Temperance, MI

One rainy Sunday afternoon, I whipped up this omelet for my husband and myself. It's now a favorite of his, even though there's no meat in it.

1/4 onion, sliced
2 to 3 t. olive oil, divided
2 eggs, beaten
1 T. sour cream
sea salt and pepper to taste

1/4 t. onion powder
1/8 t. nutmeg
1/4 c. shredded Asiago,
    Parmesan and Romano
    cheese blend

In a small skillet over medium heat, sauté onion in 2 teaspoons oil until translucent. In a small bowl, whisk together eggs, sour cream and seasonings. If necessary, add a little more oil to skillet; reduce heat to low. Pour egg mixture into skillet; swirl eggs around to fill skillet. Cook without stirring for 2 to 3 minutes, until eggs are cooked through. Add cheese to one side of skillet; fold over omelet. Allow to stand briefly until cheese melts. Serves one to 2.

Buttery cinnamon toast warms you right up on a chilly morning. Spread softened butter generously on one side of toasted white bread and sprinkle with cinnamon-sugar. Broil for one to 2 minutes until hot and bubbly. Serve with mugs of hot cocoa...yummy!

Jolly Pumpkin Oatmeal

Sandi Trader
Logan, WV

Your little goblins will eat this up! Be sure to use pumpkin pie mix in this recipe...it adds sweetness and spice that plain canned pumpkin doesn't have.

1 c. quick-cooking oats,
   uncooked
1/4 to 1 c. milk

1/2 c. canned pumpkin pie mix
2 T. raisins
Garnish: sugar

Combine oats and 1/4 cup milk in a microwave-safe bowl. Microwave on high setting one to 2 minutes, stirring once. Stir in pumpkin; stir in remaining milk as needed to reach desired consistency. Microwave an additional 30 seconds until heated through. Stir in raisins; add sugar to taste before serving. Serves 2.

Make school-day breakfasts fun! Cut the centers from
a slice of toast with a cookie cutter, serve milk or juice
with twisty straws or put a smiley face on a bagel
using raisins and cream cheese.

Applesauce Baked Oatmeal

Laura Wirsig
Holden, MO

I created this delicious recipe by making some tweaks to a recipe a friend shared with me. My husband loves this oatmeal and requests it all the time! Add more applesauce and less sugar as you wish, to suit your own taste.

1-1/2 c. quick-cooking oats, uncooked
1/4 c. sugar
1 t. baking powder
3/4 t. salt
1/2 c. milk

1/4 c. butter, softened
1 egg, beaten
1/4 c. applesauce
1 t. vanilla extract
Optional: warm milk, brown sugar, sliced fruit

Combine oats, sugar, baking powder and salt; mix well. Add remaining ingredients except optional ones; mix to a smooth, thin consistency. Spread evenly in a greased 13"x9" baking pan. Bake, uncovered, at 350 degrees for 25 to 30 minutes, until edges turn golden. Serve immediately by spooning into individual bowls. Add additional warmed milk, if needed for desired consistency. Top with brown sugar or sliced fruit, as desired. Makes 6 to 8 servings.

For a fresh fall table decoration, arrange berry-covered twigs of bittersweet in quart-size Mason jars or stoneware crocks.

Grama Ruth's Bran Muffins

Dawn Caron
Iron Mountain, MI

These bran muffins are simply delicious! I love baking my grandmother's muffins for my family because it reminds me of all the times I shared them with her. I even have the original recipe card in my own handwriting from when I was only ten years old.

1-1/4 c. all-purpose flour
1 T. baking powder
1/2 t. salt
1/2 c. sugar

2-1/2 c. bran flake cereal
1-1/4 c. milk
1 egg, beaten
1/3 c. canola oil

Stir together flour, baking powder, salt and sugar in a bowl; set aside. In a separate bowl, combine cereal and milk; let stand 2 minutes. Add egg and oil to cereal mixture; mix well. Add cereal mixture to flour mixture; stir until combined. Pour batter into greased muffin cups, filling about 2/3 full. Bake at 375 degrees for 12 to 15 minutes, until golden. Makes one dozen.

Fresh-baked muffins...sure to make sleepyheads wake right up!
Save time on busy mornings by mixing the dry ingredients
ahead of time. In the morning, just turn on the oven,
whisk in the wet ingredients, bake and serve.

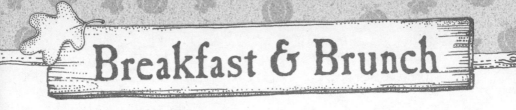

Pecan Pie Muffins

Melynda Hoffman
Fort Wayne, IN

When my daughter Brooke took these scrumptious muffins to the Allen County Fair, she won a blue ribbon. All the judges asked for another muffin...please! We make them for our holiday breakfasts, but they're a great treat anytime.

1 c. chopped pecans	2 eggs
1 c. brown sugar, packed	1/2 c. butter or coconut oil,
1/2 c. all-purpose flour	melted and cooled slightly

Mix pecans, brown sugar and flour in a large bowl; make a well in the center and set aside. In a separate bowl, beat eggs just until foam appears. Stir in butter or oil. Add pecan mixture; stir just until moistened. Spoon batter into muffin cups greased only on the bottom, filling about 2/3 full. Bake at 350 degrees for 20 to 25 minutes, until golden. Promptly remove from muffin tin; cool on a wire rack. Makes 9.

A wire basket full of brown eggs makes a terrific farm-style breakfast centerpiece. For a seasonal touch, fill the basket with colorful egg-shaped gourds.

Brown Sugar-Glazed Bacon

Caitlin Hagy
West Chester, PA

A delicious addition to any autumn breakfast table.

1 lb. bacon
1/3 c. brown sugar, packed

1 t. all-purpose flour
1/2 c. pecans, finely chopped

Place a wire rack over a baking sheet. Arrange bacon slices on rack, close together but not overlapping. In a bowl, combine remaining ingredients and sprinkle evenly over bacon. Bake at 350 degrees for about 30 minutes, until bacon is crisp and glazed. Drain on paper towels before serving. Makes 6 to 8 servings.

Wake up the family with a rise & shine omelet breakfast! Set out a variety of cheeses, vegetables and meats. Everyone can layer their favorite ingredients in a mini pie plate and get just what they want.

Breakfast & Brunch

White Cheddar Cheese Grits

Tina Goodpasture
Meadowview, VA

*Here in Virginia, we just love grits! Try this recipe and
your family will love 'em too.*

2 c. chicken broth
2 T. butter
1/2 c. quick-cooking grits,
   uncooked

1 c. shredded white Cheddar
   cheese

Bring broth and butter to a boil in a saucepan over medium heat.
Gradually whisk in grits and return to a boil. Reduce heat to medium-
low. Simmer, stirring occasionally, for 5 minutes, or until thickened.
Stir in cheese until melted. Serve immediately. Makes 4 to 6 servings.

I grew up on a farm in the Appalachian Mountains of southwest
Virginia. Like most people, we ate what we raised...chickens,
pigs, cows, sheep and of course vegetables and fruit. But the
thing I liked most was making molasses. Every September or
October we would cut the cane to start the process. It was hard
work and we would boil the juices all night long. But at the end
of all the hard work we also got to make taffy. We'd butter our
hands and have a taffy pull...boy, was it good! It was a great treat.
It is one of my fondest memories of living on a farm.

-Tina Goodpasture, Meadowview, VA

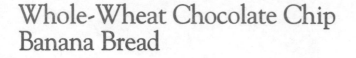

Whole-Wheat Chocolate Chip Banana Bread

Barbie Hall
Salisbury, MD

This recipe is a staple at our house. Even with the whole-wheat flour and oats it is surprisingly moist. It's an irresistible way to add these healthy ingredients to your family's diet.

3 bananas, mashed
2 eggs, beaten
1/4 c. oil
1/2 c. brown sugar, packed
1 c. whole-wheat flour

1 c. quick-cooking oats,
   uncooked
1 t. baking soda
1 c. semi-sweet chocolate chips

In a large bowl, combine bananas, eggs, oil and brown sugar. Blend well with an electric mixer on medium speed. Add flour, oats and baking soda; beat just until dry ingredients are mixed in. Stir in chocolate chips. Pour batter into a greased 9"x5" loaf pan. Bake at 350 degrees for 55 to 60 minutes. Remove bread from pan; cool completely on a wire rack. Makes one loaf.

Make a fabric liner for a basket of freshly baked bread or muffins...no sewing required! Use pinking shears to cut an 18-inch square of cotton fabric in a perky fall print. It's so simple, why not make one for the breakfast table and an extra for gift-giving?

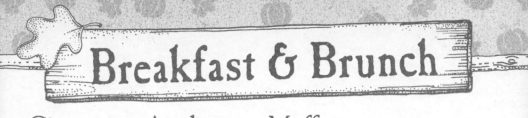

Breakfast & Brunch

Cinnamon Applesauce Muffins

Amanda Hensley
Church Hill, TN

Equally yummy at breakfast or with a warming bowl of soup.

1/2 c. butter, softened	1 t. baking soda
3/4 c. sugar	1 T. cinnamon
2 eggs, beaten	1/8 t. salt
1 t. vanilla extract	1/4 c. sour cream
1-3/4 c. all-purpose flour	1 c. applesauce
1 t. baking powder	

In a large bowl, beat butter and sugar with an electric mixer on medium speed. Beat in eggs and vanilla; set aside. In a separate bowl, mix flour, baking powder, baking soda, cinnamon and salt. Add flour mixture, sour cream and applesauce to butter mixture. Stir batter by hand until blended. Fill greased muffin cups 2/3 full. Bake at 375 degrees for 15 to 20 minutes. Makes one dozen.

For a change, try an old farmhouse tradition...a big slice of apple or pumpkin pie for breakfast!

Easy as 1-2-3 Cinnamon Rolls

Dannielle Spencer
South Solon, OH

A friend at work shared this recipe, telling me anyone can make these sweet rolls. She was right! So now my daughter requests them for breakfast all the time. Be sure to start the night before.

1/2 c. chopped pecans
20-ct. pkg. frozen dinner rolls
4-oz. pkg. instant butterscotch
   pudding mix, divided

1/2 c. brown sugar, packed
2 T. sugar
1 t. cinnamon
1/2 c. butter, melted

Sprinkle pecans in the bottom of a greased and floured 13"x9" baking pan. Arrange frozen dinner rolls on top of pecans; set aside. Measure out 1/4 cup dry pudding mix from package; reserve the remainder for a future use. In a bowl, combine 1/4 cup pudding mix, sugars and cinnamon; mix well and sprinkle over rolls. Pour melted butter evenly over pudding mixture. Let rise for 8 hours to overnight, uncovered, on kitchen counter. Bake at 325 degrees for 25 minutes. To serve, turn rolls out of pan onto a plate. Makes 20.

Spice up an autumn breakfast with cider-glazed sausages. Brown and drain a 1/2 pound of breakfast sausage links. Add a cup of apple cider to the skillet, then turn the heat down to low and simmer for 10 minutes. Yummy!

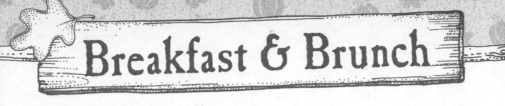

Homemade Doughnuts

Megan Brooks
Antioch, TN

Doughnuts are a BIG Halloween tradition at Grandma's house. My grandmother is eighty-five and she still makes these doughnuts for all her grandchildren and great-grandchildren when they come to her house trick-or-treating. Frightfully delicious!

2 c. biscuit baking mix	1 t. vanilla extract
1 c. sugar, divided	oil for deep frying
1/3 c. milk	1/4 t. cinnamon
1 egg, beaten	1/4 t. nutmeg

Mix together baking mix, 1/4 cup sugar, milk, egg and vanilla until well blended. Turn dough onto a lightly floured surface; knead about 10 times. Roll out to 3/8-inch thick. Cut with a floured doughnut cutter. Add oil to 3 inches depth in a heavy skillet or deep-fat fryer. Heat oil to 375 degrees over medium-high heat. Drop doughnuts into hot oil, a few at a time. Fry until golden on both sides, about one minute per side. Remove doughnuts with a slotted spoon; drain on paper towels. Combine remaining sugar and spices in a small paper bag. Add doughnuts to bag, a few at a time, and shake to coat. Serve warm. Makes about 1-1/2 dozen.

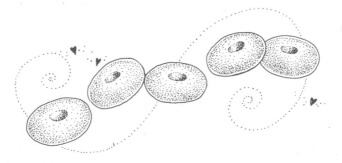

Doughnuts in a dash! For speedier homemade doughnuts, separate refrigerated biscuits and cut a hole in the center of each. Fry biscuits in hot oil until golden on both sides; drain on paper towels. Roll in sugar and serve warm.

Rita's Turkey Hash

Rita Morgan
Pueblo, CO

This is my favorite hearty breakfast to serve every Black Friday, before my sisters and I head to the mall to do some serious shopping. Add a side of leftover cranberry sauce...delish!

1 T. butter
1 T. oil
1 onion, chopped
1 red pepper, chopped
2 c. potatoes, peeled, cooked
   and diced

2 c. roast turkey, diced
1/2 t. dried thyme
salt to taste

Melt butter with oil in a large heavy skillet over medium heat. Add onion and pepper. Sauté until onion is tender, about 5 minutes. Add remaining ingredients. Spread out mixture in skillet, pressing lightly to form an even layer. Cook until golden on bottom. Using a spatula, turn over mixture (it doesn't need to stay in one piece). Cook until golden. Remove from heat. Spoon hash onto 4 plates. Top with Poached Eggs and serve immediately. Makes 4 servings.

Poached Eggs:

1 T. white vinegar
4 eggs

salt and pepper to taste

Add several inches of water to a deep skillet or saucepan. Bring water to a simmer over medium-high heat. Stir in vinegar. One at a time, crack eggs and add to water. Cook just until whites are firm and yolks are still soft, about 5 minutes. With a slotted spoon, remove eggs, one at a time. Season to taste.

Keep track of all those holiday shopping lists and recipes on a handy bulletin board! Glue a picture hanger to the back of a vintage painted metal tray, then use button magnets to hold notes in place.

Breakfast & Brunch

Make-Ahead Breakfast Casserole

Barbara Hunter Sturm
Bakersfield, CA

The ticket to a fuss-free morning when you're having a crowd for breakfast! Assemble the evening before, then just pop into the oven in the morning. Jazz it up with sautéed mushrooms, green peppers, green chiles and different flavors of croutons. Serve with a sliced fruit salad... guests will love it!

6-oz. pkg. seasoned croutons
1 lb. bacon, crisply cooked and
    crumbled
1-1/2 to 2 c. shredded Cheddar
    cheese

1 doz. eggs, beaten
1/2 c. half-and-half or milk
salt and pepper to taste

Spray a 13"x9" baking pan with non-stick vegetable spray. Arrange croutons in bottom of pan. Layer with bacon and cheese. In a bowl, beat together eggs, half-and-half or milk, salt and pepper. Pour egg mixture evenly over cheese. Cover and refrigerate overnight. Bake, uncovered, at 350 degrees for 35 minutes, or until heated through and eggs are fluffy. Serves 6 to 8.

Spoon individual servings of a savory egg casserole into toasty bread bowls. Cut the tops off round crusty bread loaves, hollow them out and brush with olive oil. Pop the bowls and lids into a 400-degree oven for 5 to 10 minutes, until crisp and golden.

Mamaw's Apple Crescent Pies

Debbie Dunham
Lumberton, TX

*Wonderful for breakfast...speedy enough for a quick dessert
any time pop-in guests arrive!*

8-oz. tube refrigerated crescent
  rolls
1/2 c. sugar
1 t. cinnamon

1 Granny Smith apple, cored
  and cut into 8 slices
Optional: 1/2 c. chopped nuts
Garnish: whipped cream

Separate crescent rolls and place on a baking sheet sprayed with
non-stick vegetable spray. Combine sugar and cinnamon; sprinkle
evenly over rolls. Place one apple slice on each roll. Sprinkle with
nuts, if desired. Roll up crescent-style. Bake at 375 degrees for 14 to
16 minutes, until golden. Serve warm, topped with whipped cream.
Serves 4.

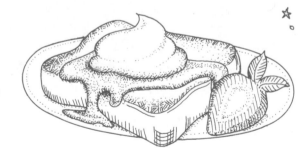

Whip up a luscious topping to dollop on pancakes, French toast
and slices of fruit bread....yum! Combine 3/4 cup whipping
cream, 2 tablespoons softened cream cheese and one tablespoon
powdered sugar. Beat with an electric mixer on medium speed
until soft peaks form. Keep refrigerated in a small covered crock.

Breakfast & Brunch

Quick Cheese Danish

Virginia Arbisi
Elmont, NY

Turn this into a fruit & cheese Danish in a jiffy! Spread a small can of pastry fruit filling over the cream cheese mixture.

2 8-oz. tubes refrigerated
   crescent rolls
2 8-oz. pkgs. cream cheese,
   softened

1-1/4 c. sugar, divided
1 t. vanilla extract
1 t. cinnamon
1/2 c. butter, melted

Unroll one tube of crescent rolls and place in the bottom of a lightly greased 13"x9" baking pan. In a large bowl, beat cream cheese, one cup sugar and vanilla until creamy; spread mixture over rolls. Unroll second tube of rolls and layer over cream cheese mixture. Mix remaining sugar with cinnamon; sprinkle over rolls. Drizzle with melted butter. Bake at 350 degrees for 30 to 35 minutes. Cut into squares. Makes 12 to 15 servings.

We have a fun family gift exchange that we call our Yard Sale Swap. At the first summer picnic of every year, family members draw names (shh...it's a secret!). Then you hit the yard sales and tag sales to find a gift that costs no more than five dollars for the person whose name you drew. At the last picnic of the year, which is usually in October, we exchange our gifts. It's a lot of fun for very little money.

-Virginia Hagerman, Jolo, WV

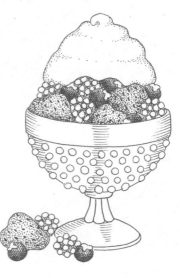

Crustless Ham & Spinach Quiche
Tracie Daugherty
Kittanning, PA

My family enjoys this satisfying egg dish for breakfast, lunch or dinner.
It's good either warm or cold, travels well and freezes very nicely.
What more could you want?

1 doz. eggs
2 c. whipping cream or milk
1/2 t. garlic powder
1/2 t. dried oregano
1/8 t. pepper

1 c. cooked ham, finely diced
10-oz. pkg. frozen spinach,
  thawed and drained
1/4 to 1/2 c. onion, finely diced
2 c. shredded Cheddar cheese

In a large bowl, with an electric mixer on low speed, beat eggs and cream or milk well. Stir in seasonings with a spoon; set aside. Sprinkle remaining ingredients evenly into a 13"x9" baking pan sprayed with non-stick vegetable spray. Slowly pour egg mixture into pan. Bake, uncovered, at 350 degrees for 45 to 50 minutes, until golden and a knife tip inserted in center tests clean. Allow to cool slightly before cutting into squares. Makes 8 servings.

A breakfast trifle! Layer creamy yogurt, crunchy granola and juicy fresh berries in a clear glass bowl... perfect for brunch guests with lighter appetites.

Breakfast & Brunch

Sticky Bun Toast Topper

Irene Robinson
Cincinnati, OH

A special way to dress up plain toast...it goes together in a jiffy!

2 T. brown sugar, packed
1 T. butter
1 T. light corn syrup

1/4 t. cinnamon
4 slices white bread, toasted
1/4 c. chopped pecans, toasted

Combine brown sugar, butter, corn syrup and cinnamon in a glass measuring cup. Microwave on high setting for one minute. Stir; spread evenly over toast slices. Sprinkle with pecans. Makes 4 servings.

Set a pillar candle in a canning jar that's partially filled with candy corn, whole cranberries or acorns...it sets a fall mood instantly for any breakfast table!

Tex-Mex Egg Puff

Carol Creed
Battlefield, MO

I experimented with the ingredients until this recipe was just right!
Mix, bake and serve, how easy is that?

1 doz. eggs, beaten
2 4-oz. cans chopped mild
   green chiles
16-oz. pkg. shredded Monterey
   Jack cheese
16-oz. container small-curd
   cream-style cottage cheese

1/2 c. butter, melted and cooled
   slightly
1/2 c. all-purpose flour
1 t. baking powder
1/2 t. salt

In a large bowl, mix all ingredients together. Pour into a greased
13"x9" glass baking pan. Bake, uncovered, at 350 degrees for 35 to
40 minutes, until set. Cut into squares. Serves 8 to 10.

Take your family to a nearby park at sunrise for a breakfast picnic
filled with rosy skies and singing birds...you'll have the park all to
yourselves! Tote along a warm breakfast casserole, a basket of
muffins and thermoses of coffee and hot chocolate...perfect for
making memories together.

Vickie's Favorite Guacamole

Vickie

Whenever we have a Mexican-themed potluck here at
Gooseberry Patch, *I'm requested to bring my guacamole.*
It's almost foolproof and oh-so-good!

4 avocados, halved and pitted
1 onion, chopped
2 cloves garlic, minced
2 T. lime juice
1/8 t. kosher salt
tortilla chips

Scoop pulp out of avocados into a bowl. Mash to desired consistency
with a potato masher. Add remaining ingredients; mix well. Serve
with your favorite tortilla chips. Makes 2 cups.

Use tiered cake stands for bite-size appetizers...so handy, and
they take up less space on the buffet table than setting out
several serving platters. Don't have a cake stand? Simply turn
over a large sturdy bowl and balance a platter atop it.

Easy Mexican Dip

Donna Scheletsky
Baden, PA

This simple recipe has been a favorite at our tailgate parties when we attend the local bi-annual community musical. All our friends take over the entire parking lot of the fire hall and enjoy snacks and beverages before the play, during intermission and afterwards! The money raised by the performances goes to our all-volunteer fire department. It's a great cause and a lot of fun!

8-oz. pkg. cream cheese, softened
2 T. taco seasoning mix, or more to taste
1/4 c. tomato juice
tortilla chips

In a bowl, mix together cream cheese and taco seasoning. Add tomato juice; stir to desired dipping consistency. Serve with tortilla chips. Makes 8 to 10 servings.

Make a fluffy fabric garland to celebrate the season. Use pinking shears to cut strips of fabric, about 6 inches long and 1/2 inch wide. Cut a piece of thick jute the length you'd like the garland to be, then tie on the fabric strips with a simple knot. A mix of colors and prints is pleasing...try team colors for a tailgating party or black and orange for Halloween!

Creamy Pumpkin Spread

Sheila Gwaltney
Johnson City, TN

Perfect for fall get-togethers...everyone raves about it!

8-oz. pkg. cream cheese,
   softened
7-oz. jar marshmallow creme
1/2 c. canned pumpkin

1/4 t. cinnamon
1/4 t. nutmeg
shortbread cookies, graham
   crackers, gingersnaps

Combine all ingredients except cookies; mix until well blended. Cover and refrigerate for 3 to 4 hours before serving. Serve with cookies or graham crackers for dipping. Makes 2-1/2 cups.

Great Pumpkin Dip

Jenny Sarbacker
Madison, WI

My version of a recipe I found years ago. It's always a hit!

15-oz. can pumpkin
15-oz. jar creamy peanut butter
1-1/2 c. brown sugar, packed
2 t. vanilla extract

1/8 t. cinnamon
1/8 t. nutmeg
apple slices

In a large bowl, mix all ingredients except apples until smooth. Cover and refrigerate at least 30 minutes before serving. Serve with apple slices. Serves 10.

For a yummy lunchbox treat, tuck in a covered container of creamy dip along with some fresh fruit or veggie dippers.

Snacks & Appetizers

Spicy-Sweet Pumpkin Pie Dip

Krista Smith
Dayton, OH

*I make this for Thanksgiving gatherings and carry-ins and
am always asked for the recipe!*

2 8-oz. pkgs. cream cheese,
　softened
4 c. powdered sugar
15-oz. can pumpkin

2 t. cinnamon
1 t. ground ginger
gingersnaps, vanilla wafers,
　graham crackers

Mix together cream cheese and powdered sugar in a large bowl until
well blended. Add remaining ingredients except cookies; mix well.
Cover and refrigerate. Serve with gingersnaps, vanilla wafers or
graham crackers. Serves 12 to 16.

Pumpkin Patch Dip

Anne Ptacik
Yuma, CO

*This recipe is a great way to use leftover pumpkin. It tastes yummy
and always makes me think of autumn, my favorite season.*

8-oz. pkg. cream cheese,
　softened
3/4 c. canned pumpkin
1 c. finely shredded Cheddar
　cheese
1 T. brown sugar, packed

1/4 t. cinnamon
1/4 t. allspice
1/4 t. nutmeg
assorted snack crackers,
　vegetable slices

Mix all ingredients together except crackers and vegetables in a bowl.
Stir until well-combined and smooth. Cover and refrigerate. Serve with
assorted crackers and vegetables. Makes about 2 cups.

Pork & Apple Meatballs

Emmaline Dunkley
Pine City, MN

These have been a big hit at office potluck parties! Serve immediately or keep warm in a slow cooker until ready to serve.

1 lb. ground pork sausage
1-1/4 c. pork-flavored stuffing
   mix
1/2 c. low-sodium chicken broth
1/2 c. Honeycrisp apple, peeled,
   cored and diced

1/2 c. onion, diced
1 egg, beaten
1-1/2 t. mustard
1/2 c. shredded sharp Cheddar
   cheese

In a large bowl, combine all ingredients. Form into balls by tablespoonfuls. Place on a 15"x10" jelly-roll pan coated with non-stick vegetable spray. Bake at 350 degrees for 18 to 20 minutes, until meatballs are no longer pink in the middle. Serves 8 to 10.

My favorite fall tradition is our town's festival in October. Everyone comes home for Fort Days, even if they don't come home for Thanksgiving or Christmas. The center of town is shut down for the festival's food and craft booths, all within walking distance. There's a big community parade that goes on for two hours. My favorite festival memory is from 2008, our town's 250th anniversary, when the National Anthem was sung for the opening ceremony. No one said a word, just listening to the man who sang it. It was very moving, as if time had stopped.

-Pam West, Ligonier, PA

Savory Party Loaf

Irene Robinson
Cincinnati, OH

*It's impossible to stop nibbling on warm pieces of
this cheesy, oniony bread...yum!*

1 round loaf sourdough bread
1 lb. Monterey Jack cheese,
   sliced

1/2 c. butter, melted
1/2 c. green onion, chopped
2 to 3 t. poppy seed

Score bread lengthwise and crosswise without cutting through the
bottom. Insert cheese slices between cuts. Combine remaining
ingredients and drizzle over bread. Wrap loaf in aluminum foil; place
on an ungreased baking sheet. Bake at 350 degrees for 15 minutes.
Unwrap loaf and return to oven. Bake an additional 10 minutes,
uncovered, until cheese is melted. Makes 10 to 15 servings.

Throw a pumpkin painting party! Provide acrylic paints,
brushes and plenty of pumpkins...invite kids to bring
their imagination and an old shirt to wear as a smock.
Parents are sure to join in too!

Sticky-Sweet Caramel Apples

Melody Taynor
Everett, WA

I like to use the smallest apples I can find and make 'em mini...so cute for party favors! You'll be able to make 10 to 12 mini apples with this recipe.

4 to 6 wooden treat sticks
4 to 6 Gala or Jonagold apples
14-oz. pkg. caramels,
  unwrapped

2 T. milk
Optional: candy sprinkles,
  chopped nuts, mini
  candy-coated chocolates

Insert sticks into apples; set aside. Combine caramels and milk in a microwave-safe bowl. Microwave, uncovered, for 2 minutes, stirring once. Allow to cool briefly. Roll each apple quickly in caramel, turning to coat. Set apples to dry on lightly greased wax paper. When partially set, roll in toppings, if desired. Makes 4 to 6.

Stir up some old-fashioned fun this Halloween. Light the house with spooky candlelight and serve homemade popcorn balls, pumpkin cookies and hot cider. Bob for apples and play pin the tail on the black cat...kids of all ages will love it!

Homemade Gummy Worms

Heidi Jakubiak
Chrisman, IL

This is such fun to do with my kids and we love to eat them when they're ready. Hope you enjoy trying it! If you're a real candy connoisseur, you might like to make these in candy molds for fancier gummy candy.

1 c. boiling water
2 .3-oz. pkgs. favorite-flavor
   sugar-free gelatin mix

2 .3-oz. pkgs. favorite-flavor
   unsweetened drink mix
3 1-oz. envs. unflavored gelatin

Coat an 8"x8" baking pan with non-stick vegetable spray; set aside. In a bowl, combine all ingredients and stir until dissolved. Pour into prepared pan. Cover and refrigerate for 2 to 3 hours, until completely set. Cut into 1/4-inch wide strips to form thin "worms" for serving as is or decorating other treats. Makes about 2-1/2 dozen.

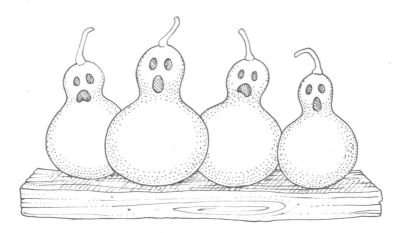

Create a spooky greeting for trick-or-treaters...it's simple!
Paint a dried bottle gourd white and use a black felt tip pen to
add a ghostly face. Line up several along the mantel.

Chili-Lime Pecans

Sharon Jones
Oklahoma City, OK

*These spicy nuts for nibbling are very easy to make and
are enjoyed at all kinds of get-togethers. I usually double this
recipe, to make sure I'll have enough!*

2 T. lime juice
1 T. olive oil
1 t. paprika
1 t. sea salt

1 t. chili powder
1/2 t. cayenne pepper
3 c. pecan halves

In a bowl, stir together all ingredients except pecans. Add pecans and
toss to coat well. Spread pecans in an aluminum foil-lined, lightly
greased 15"x10" jelly-roll pan. Bake at 350 degrees for 12 to
14 minutes, until pecans are toasted and dry, stirring occasionally.
Cool completely; store in an airtight container. Makes 3 cups.

Take the family to a small-town parade for real hometown spirit.
Marching bands, horse-drawn wagons and antique cars...what
fun! Remember to tote along a blanket to sit on, a snack for
munching and some mini flags for the kids to wave.

Snackin' Pumpkin Seeds

Suzanne Bayorgeon
Norfolk, NY

Every Halloween we carve pumpkins...I can't resist doing something yummy with all those seeds!

2 c. pumpkin seeds
3 T. butter, melted

1-1/4 t. salt
1/2 t. Worcestershire sauce

In an ungreased shallow baking pan, combine all ingredients; stir to mix. Bake at 250 degrees for about 2 hours, stirring occasionally, until seeds are crisp, dry and golden. Cool completely; store in an airtight container. Makes 2 cups.

Give your fireplace a welcoming autumn glow, even if Indian summer weather has made it too warm for an actual fire! Fill it with pots of flame-colored orange and yellow mums or marigolds.

Queen's Cheddar-Onion Dip

Traci Beck
Howard, PA

This is something I always serve when having "the girls" over.
We feel like queens eating such a rich and velvety treat!

1 c. mayonnaise
1 c. shredded extra-sharp
   Cheddar cheese

1 onion, chopped
nacho-flavored tortilla chips

Mix together all ingredients except tortilla chips. Place in a lightly greased one-quart casserole dish. Bake, uncovered, at 350 degrees for 35 to 40 minutes, until it bubbles. Let cool 5 to 10 minutes; serve warm with tortilla chips. Serves 6.

Fran's Potato Chip Dip

Fran Bodenhamer
Gillette, WY

I make this dip year 'round...for Halloween, Christmas and other party occasions. My husband and daughter always ask, "Are you ever going to make this just for us?"

8-oz. pkg. cream cheese,
   softened
1/4 c. mayonnaise-type salad
   dressing

garlic powder to taste
1-1/2 to 2 T. Worcestershire
   sauce
1 T. sweet pickle juice

Combine all ingredients in a bowl. Beat together for several minutes, blending well. Keep refrigerated until serving time. Makes 1-1/2 to 2 cups.

A hollowed-out squash or pumpkin
is a fun way to serve favorite
dips...place it on a serving tray
and surround with a variety of
crackers and veggie dippers.

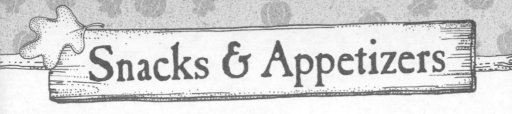
Laurie's Cheesy Bean Dip

Sharon Lampman
Clawson, MI

My co-worker Laurie brought this simple slow-cooker dip to one of our staff luncheons and I fell in love with it. The next day, I took this new-found yummy dip along to a friend's housewarming party. All I heard was, "Wow, this is good!" So I asked Laurie if I could submit it to my favorite cookbook company...she said "Sure!" and here it is!

2 11-1/2 oz. cans bean with
   bacon soup
16-oz. container sour cream

1 c. shredded Cheddar cheese
2 t. taco seasoning mix
tortilla chips

In a slow cooker, blend all ingredients except tortilla chips. Cover and cook on high setting for 2 hours, or until dip is warm and bubbly. Turn down to low setting to keep warm; serve with tortilla chips. Makes 10 to 12 servings.

Decorate a grapevine garland to wind around the front door.
Garland can be found at craft stores...use orange or yellow raffia
to tie on gourds, mini Indian corn and dried seed pods.
It'll look welcoming all autumn long.

Parmesan Shortbread Crisps

JoAnn

These crisp, flavorful rounds bake up in a jiffy. They're tasty with bowls of hot soup or with your favorite herbed cheese spread.

1-3/4 c. all-purpose flour
3/4 c. plus 2 T. grated Parmesan cheese, divided
1/2 clove garlic, minced

1 t. salt
1/8 t. cayenne pepper
1 c. chilled butter, cubed

In a food processor, mix together flour, 3/4 cup Parmesan cheese, garlic and seasonings. Add butter; process until dough begins to form. Form dough into a ball; divide in half. Shape each half into a 12-inch log. Slice logs into one-inch pieces; roll each piece into a ball. Arrange on parchment paper-lined baking sheets, 1-1/2 inches apart. Flatten each ball into a 2-inch circle; sprinkle with remaining cheese. Bake at 350 degrees for 20 minutes, or until dry on top and dry and golden on the bottom. Transfer to a wire rack; cool completely. Store in an airtight container. Makes 2 dozen.

For super-simple cheese snacks, cut several 8-ounce packages of cream cheese into 10 cubes each. Shape cubes into balls and roll in snipped fresh parsley or chopped pecans. Easy to make ahead...just arrange on a plate, cover and pop in the fridge until party time.

Pizza Roll Snacks

Diane Cohen
The Woodlands, TX

Who needs frozen pizza rolls when it's a snap to make these yummy rolls? My girls love these for after-school snacks. If there are leftovers, they warm up great in the microwave.

8-oz. tube refrigerated crescent
   rolls
1/3 c. pizza sauce
1/4 c. grated Parmesan cheese

16 slices pepperoni, divided
1/3 c. shredded mozzarella
   cheese, divided

Unroll rolls but do not separate; press perforations to seal. Spread pizza sauce evenly over rolls, leaving a one-inch border. Sprinkle with Parmesan cheese. Roll up dough jelly-roll fashion, starting with the short side. Using a sharp knife, cut into 15 slices. Place slices cut-side down on a greased baking sheet. Top each slice with one pepperoni slice and one teaspoon mozzarella cheese. Bake at 375 degrees for 9 to 11 minutes, or until edges are golden and cheese is melted. Makes 16 servings.

Bite-size mini sandwiches make an easy, tasty addition to any appetizer buffet. Whip up some grilled cheese, BLT, Reuben or other favorite sandwiches, then cut them into small squares. Top with an olive or a pickle slice and spear with party picks.

Pub Beer Dip

Karen Hazelett
Fremont, IN

We enjoy the time we spend at Lake James in northeast Indiana. Winters at the lake are lonely for year 'rounders, so we started a monthly card club with five other couples. It's a terrific way to see your neighbors during colder months and try each other's recipes. Our friend Jan is a wonderful hostess and shared this slow-cooker recipe with us. It was an immediate hit!

2 5-oz. jars sharp Cheddar
   cheese spread
8-oz. pkg. cream cheese,
   softened
1/2 c. regular or non-alcoholic
   beer

1 t. Worcestershire sauce
5 to 6 drops hot pepper sauce
4 to 5 slices bacon, crisply
   cooked and crumbled
pretzels, crackers, bread slices

In a 2-1/2 to 3-quart slow cooker, mix together cheeses, beer and sauces. Cover and cook on low setting for 2 hours, stirring occasionally. Dip will become thicker the longer it cooks. Stir in bacon just before serving. Serve with pretzels, crackers or bread. Makes about 4 cups.

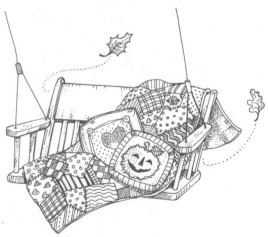

Make the most of your front porch! A porch swing, rocking chairs, comfy pillows and hanging baskets of fall flowers create a cozy place for family & friends to visit and enjoy the crisp air.

TNT Dip

Teresa Stiegelmeyer
Indianapolis, IN

*Make this peppery slow-cooker dip even spicer by adding hot pepper
sauce to taste or using extra-hot salsa...if you dare!*

1-1/2 lbs. ground beef, browned
   and drained
10-3/4 oz. can cream of
   mushroom soup
1 c. salsa

1/4 c. butter, melted
2 T. chili powder
16-oz. pkg. pasteurized process
   cheese spread, cubed
corn chips, party rye bread

In a large saucepan over medium heat, combine all ingredients
except chips and bread. Cook and stir until bubbly and cheese is
melted. If preferred, combine all ingredients except chips and bread in
a slow cooker. Cover and cook on high setting for about one hour,
stirring occasionally. Serve with corn chips or party rye bread.
Serves 10 to 12.

Treat yourself to a jolly jack-o'-lantern shake! Add 3 scoops
vanilla ice cream, 2 tablespoons canned pumpkin, 1/4 cup milk
and 1/4 teaspoon pumpkin pie spice to a blender. Blend until
smooth. Pour into two tall glasses and share with a friend.

Goblin Good Snack Mix

Denise Oravecz
Pittsburgh, PA

Family, friends and co-workers love "goblin" up this yummy snack mix! I make it for Halloween parties, fall gatherings and even for Thanksgiving.

4 c. bite-size crispy cereal
  squares
4 c. popped kettle corn or
  regular popcorn
1 c. honey-roasted peanuts
1 c. salted roasted pumpkin
  seeds

1/4 c. butter
6 T. brown sugar, packed
2 T. light corn syrup
1/4 t. vanilla extract
1/4 t. pumpkin pie spice
1 c. candy corn and/or candy
  pumpkins

In a 4-quart microwave-safe bowl, mix cereal, popcorn, peanuts and pumpkin seeds; set aside. In a microwave-safe bowl, combine butter, brown sugar, corn syrup and vanilla. Microwave, uncovered, on high setting for about 2 minutes, until mixture is boiling; stir after one minute. Stir in spice. Pour over cereal mixture and stir until evenly coated. Microwave 5 minutes, stirring after every minute. Spread on wax paper. Let cool for about 15 minutes, stirring occasionally to break up any large pieces. Add candy and toss to mix. Store in an airtight container. Makes about 11 cups.

For crunchy variety in autumn snacking, try Mexican pumpkin seeds, called "pepitas." They're available year 'round in the Mexican food section of most grocery stores.

Super-Simple Candy Mix

Denise Neal
Castle Rock, CO

I got this little recipe from a lady while we were waiting in line at the grocery store. It's my favorite treat to toss together for Halloween or bunko parties...a yummy combo that tastes like a candy bar!

1 c. candy-coated chocolates   1 c. candy corn
1 c. salted peanuts

Mix ingredients together in a serving bowl and serve. Makes 3 cups.

Our family has a fun craft we do every fall...we call it Haunted Halloween Heads! I save lots of juice and water jugs and bottles in all sizes. We spray-paint them in fun, spooky colors and paint faces directly on some of the bottles. For others, I have my husband cut small circles for faces out of wood and we attach them to the bottles for a 3-D look. Finally, we glue on raffia for hair. When we're done, we dig little holes in our front garden and bury the necks of the bottles so it looks like a haunted graveyard. We like to decorate bricks for little tombstone markers with funny sayings like "Barry A. Live."
It's a cute twist on a silly Halloween!

-Kelly Lowry, Johnstown, CO

Oh-So-Easy Apple Cider

Teri Johnson
Montezuma, IA

My daughters ask for this warm-you-up beverage every year.
I sometimes put it in a percolator coffeepot...its spicy aroma makes
the whole house smell yummy!

3 qts. apple juice
2 qts. cranberry juice cocktail

1/2 c. brown sugar, packed
4 4-inch cinnamon sticks

Mix all ingredients together in a large stockpot. Simmer over low heat
until hot; keep warm. Makes about 40 servings.

There's a funny little fellow
Sitting out on our fence
And you know who I mean.
He came last night from Pumpkintown
To spend the Halloween.

-Old children's song

56

Apricot-Apple Harvest Brew

Kelly Gillow
Easton, PA

Just as the trees begin to show off their radiant autumn colors and there's a chill in the air, I look forward to serving up this warm & cozy harvest brew in my home and my country store. My family, friends and customers look forward to this drink every fall...I've shared many copies of the recipe!

1 gal. apple cider
11-1/2 oz. can apricot nectar
1 c. sugar
2 c. orange juice
3/4 c. lemon juice

4 4-inch cinnamon sticks
2 t. allspice
1 t. ground cloves
1/2 t. nutmeg

Bring all ingredients to a boil in a large stockpot over medium heat. Reduce heat; simmer for about 10 minutes. Makes about 20 servings.

For tasty fun at your next game-day party, turn any favorite Cheddar cheese ball recipe into a "football." Just shape, sprinkle with paprika and pipe on sour cream or cream cheese "laces"...so easy!

Peanut Butter-Banana Roll-Up

Wendy Ball
Battle Creek, MI

As a healthy treat for young children, I modified a favorite snack that I just love. I have made this for my children and now my grandson and nephews. It's a super busy-day snack!

10-inch whole-wheat flour
    tortilla
1/4 c. crunchy or creamy peanut
    butter

1 banana, thinly sliced
Optional: 2 to 3 T. fruit jam or
    marshmallow creme

Spread tortilla with peanut butter all the way to the edge. Arrange banana slices over peanut butter in a single layer. If desired, dollop with jam or marshmallow creme. Roll up tortilla with the seam on the bottom. You can either serve it immediately or warm it up for 30 seconds in the microwave. Serves one.

That first crackling fire and scent of wood smoke tell us it's fall! Gather lots of games and puzzles for cozy nights at home with family & friends.

Elephant Ears

Tonya Adams
Magnolia, KY

I used to love eating these sweet, golden rounds of dough at the county fair, so I joined 4-H and learned to make them myself!

1/4 c. sugar
1 t. cinnamon
10-oz. tube refrigerated biscuits,
   separated

oil for frying

Combine sugar and cinnamon in a small bowl; set aside. For each elephant ear, press 2 biscuits together. Roll out between 2 sheets of wax paper until as thin as possible. Add enough oil to a large skillet to cover the bottom. Over medium heat, fry elephant ears, one at a time, until golden on one side. Flip gently and fry the other side. Drain on paper towels. Sprinkle with sugar mixture; serve warm. Makes 5 servings.

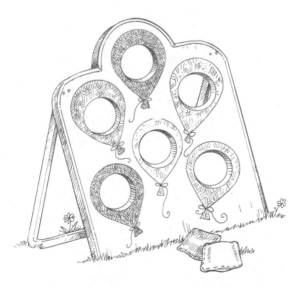

Invite friends and neighbors over for a backyard festival on a sunny autumn day. Games like a hay bale toss, sack races, Red Rover and three-legged races add old-fashioned fun!

Hot Ham & Cheddar Dip

Jessica Branch
Colchester, IL

A hearty warm-you-up snack for fall.

2 8-oz. pkgs. cream cheese,
   softened
1 onion, diced
1 lb. cooked ham, diced

1 t. garlic salt
4 c. shredded mild Cheddar
   cheese, divided
tortilla chips, crackers

Blend together cream cheese, onion, ham, garlic salt and cheese, reserving 1/4 cup cheese for topping. Spread in a greased 2-quart casserole dish; sprinkle with reserved cheese. Bake at 350 degrees for 20 minutes, or until warmed through and cheese has melted. Serve with tortilla chips and crackers. Makes 4 cups.

A striking autumn bouquet is as close as your own backyard!
While you're raking up fallen leaves, keep an eye out for short
branches of colorful leaves, late-blooming flowers and
interesting bare twigs to arrange in a tall vase.

Snacks & Appetizers

Dad's Zippy Cheese Dip

Cynthia Anderson
Mantua, OH

This was my father's special recipe. We always kidded him that
he never measured anything and just dumped it all together.
It was always delicious, though!

2 cloves garlic, pressed
1 onion, minced
1/4 c. catsup
1 T. Worcestershire sauce
2 8-oz. pkgs. cream cheese,
   softened

2 5-oz. jars sharp Cheddar
   cheese spread
crackers, chips, vegetable slices

Place garlic, onion, catsup and Worcestershire sauce in a blender or
food processor; blend well. Add cream cheese and blend; add cheese
spread, one jar at at a time, and blend until smooth. Transfer to a
serving bowl. Cover and refrigerate for one hour or more. Serve with
crackers, chips or vegetables. Makes 12 servings.

Cherry tomatoes make yummy party nibbles. Cut off the top of
each tomato, scoop out seeds with a small melon baller and
turn over to drain on paper towels. Pipe softened cream cheese
or a favorite creamy dip into hollowed tomatoes and
sprinkle fresh parsley over top.

Rainbow Popcorn

Jill Ball
Highland, UT

This is an easy, fun treat! Use any color of food coloring you like...orange for Halloween, your team's colors or your child's favorite color for a birthday party.

8 c. popped popcorn
1/2 c. milk
2 c. sugar

1 t. vanilla extract
few drops desired food coloring

Completely coat the inside of a large brown paper bag with non-stick vegetable spray. Place popcorn in bag; set aside. In a heavy saucepan, combine milk and sugar. Bring to a boil over medium heat, being careful not to let it burn. Do not scrape the sides of the pan, or the sugar will crystallize. Add vanilla and food coloring; mix well. Pour milk mixture over popcorn in bag. Close bag and shake to coat popcorn evenly. Spread popcorn on a baking sheet to dry. Store in airtight containers. Makes about 8 cups.

Pick up some plastic icing cones when you shop for baking supplies. Filled with party mix, tied with curling ribbon and placed in a wire cupcake stand, they make fun gifts to keep on hand for drop-in guests.

Party Popcorn Balls

Marie Yoder
Hudson, MI

I used to make these scrumptious goodies for my children by the bushelful whenever they'd have a fall gathering or hayride. You can substitute any flavor of gelatin you wish.

16 to 20 c. popped popcorn
1 c. light corn syrup
1/2 c. sugar

3-oz. pkg. strawberry gelatin mix

Place popcorn in a very large heatproof bowl; set aside. Mix together remaining ingredients in a saucepan over medium heat. Bring to a boil. Cool slightly; pour over popcorn. Stir well. Working quickly, with well-buttered hands, form popcorn mixture into balls. Wrap each ball in plastic wrap. Makes about one dozen.

Mix up some mulling spice bags to have on hand when chilly weather arrives. Fill a small drawstring muslin bag with one teaspoon each of whole cloves, allspice and orange zest plus two or three cinnamon sticks. Simmer the spice bag in 2 quarts apple cider for a hot, bubbly beverage that will warm you right up.

Claudia's Famous Wing Dip

Jason Keller
Carrollton, GA

My wife Claudia makes a triple batch for me to take tailgating with the guys every October. They've threatened to leave me behind if I don't bring it...that's how good it is!

8-oz. pkg. cream cheese,
  softened
16-oz. container sour cream
1 c. blue cheese salad dressing
1/2 c. hot wing sauce

2-1/2 c. cooked chicken,
  shredded
1 c. provolone cheese, shredded
tortilla chips, celery sticks

In a large bowl, beat cream cheese, sour cream, salad dressing and wing sauce until well blended. Stir in chicken and cheese. Transfer to a greased 2-quart casserole dish. Cover and bake at 350 degrees for 25 to 30 minutes, until hot and bubbly. Serve warm with tortilla chips and celery sticks. Makes 6-1/2 cups.

Do you love tailgating but can't score tickets to the big stadium football game? Tailgating at the local Friday-night high school game can be just as much fun...round up the gang, pack a picnic and cheer on your team!

Dee's Buffalo Dip

Deanna Lyons
Roswell, GA

This yummy dip is oh-so easy to make and incredibly delicious...you will never have leftovers. Surprise...it's low-fat too!

2 10-oz. cans white chicken, drained and flaked
2 8-oz. pkgs. Neufchâtel cheese, softened
1 c. low-fat ranch salad dressing
3/4 c. hot pepper sauce
2 c. shredded reduced-fat Cheddar cheese, divided
assorted vegetables, crackers

In a microwave-safe bowl, combine chicken and Neufchâtel cheese. Microwave, uncovered, on high setting for 45 seconds. Blend well. Add salad dressing, hot sauce and one cup Cheddar cheese; mix well. Transfer to a lightly greased 8"x8" baking pan. Sprinkle reserved cheese on top. Bake, uncovered, at 350 degrees for 25 to 30 minutes, until hot and bubbly. Serve with assorted vegetables or crackers. Makes 8 to 10 servings.

Serve crunchy homemade tortilla chips with your favorite salsa! Simply cut corn tortillas with seasonal cookie cutters...how about footballs, ghosts or autumn leaves? Spritz cut-outs with non-stick vegetable spray and arrange on an ungreased baking sheet. Sprinkle with salt and bake at 350 degrees until crisp, 5 to 10 minutes. Try seasoned salt or garlic salt for an extra kick.

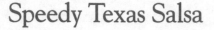

Speedy Texas Salsa

Colleen Trenholm
Salado, TX

*My mom gave me this recipe twenty-five years ago. We both
still enjoy making it. Everyone always wants the recipe
and can't believe how easy it is to make!*

28-oz. can diced tomatoes
1/4 c. onion, chopped
1/4 c. fresh cilantro
2 cloves garlic, chopped

1/2 to 1 whole canned jalapeño
   pepper
1/2 t. garlic salt
1/2 t. seasoned salt

Combine undrained tomatoes and remaining ingredients in a blender.
Blend until well mixed. Serve immediately or chill until serving time.
Makes about 4 cups.

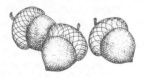

Forty years ago this October, my two daughters and I met my
four soon-to-be "new" children for the first time. Tom and I had
been dating awhile and decided it was time to get our families
acquainted. We planned a picnic for the eight of us and our
parents too. Before we began grilling the hamburgers and hot
dogs, we decided to play a game of tag football. Autumn leaves
were everywhere, crunching under our feet. At one point
I got the ball and it became evident that I was to be "buried" in
those leaves. All six kids played the Bury-Sherry game with
great glee. The crisp autumn day was glorious and so much fun.
But, the best part was realizing that I had been accepted.
We have been a wonderfully blended family now for over
thirty-five years and Tom and I have fifteen grandchildren
with whom to share another autumn!

-Sherry Huxtable, Wichita, KS

Jalapeño-Cheese Squares

Jo Ann Garcia
Alpine, TX

An acquaintance brought this wonderful dish for a luncheon one day. Everyone fell in love with its zesty taste! Increase or decrease the jalapeño peppers to your preference.

2 c. shredded Cheddar cheese
2 c. shredded Monterey Jack
  cheese
3/4 c. pickled jalapeño pepper
  slices

2 eggs, beaten
1/2 c. all-purpose flour
12-oz. can evaporated milk

Mix together cheeses; spread half of mixture in a greased 13"x9" baking pan. Top with peppers; sprinkle remaining cheese mixture over top. In a bowl, stir together eggs, flour and evaporated milk. Pour over cheese mixture. Bake, uncovered, at 350 degrees for 25 to 30 minutes, until hot and cheese is melted. Let cool slightly before cutting into squares. Serves 4 to 6.

Dress up a party table with "pumpkins" made of bright orange crysanthemums. Trim the stems of real or silk mums to one inch and insert the stems into a large styrofoam ball until it's completely covered. Add a cluster of green leaves at the top for the pumpkin "stem." Balance several pumpkin balls atop stemmed glasses...so eye-catching!

Graveyard Crunch

Kerry Mayer
Dunham Springs, LA

Our Halloween celebration wouldn't be the same without this tasty spooky treat! I like to give away small paper treat bags filled with Graveyard Crunch to party-goers, complete with tombstones drawn on the front and names, dates and silly messages scratched on them.

1/4 c. pancake syrup
2 T. butter, softened
1/4 t. cinnamon
4 c. cocoa-flavored crispy
   rice cereal

1 c. dry-roasted peanuts
2 c. mini marshmallows
1 c. candy corn
1 c. candy-coated chocolates

Mix syrup, butter and cinnamon in a large microwave-safe bowl. Microwave, uncovered, on high setting for one minute; stir until butter is completely melted. Add cereal and peanuts; toss to mix. Spread on a lightly greased 15"x10" jelly-roll pan. Bake at 300 degrees for 30 minutes, stirring after 15 minutes. Cool completely. Break into pieces; toss with remaining ingredients. Store in an airtight container. Makes 9 cups.

Mummy's the word! Whip up some fun treat containers in a jiffy. Glue wiggly eyes to the front of clear plastic drink cups, then wind cotton gauze around & around, fastening at both ends with a little glue...clever!

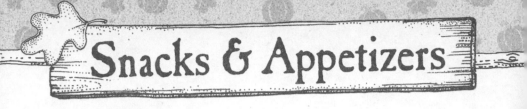

Monster Munch

Sandy Groezinger
Stockton, IL

I've made this irresistible crunchy mix for my daughter's class parties for many years. My son couldn't wait to take it for his class parties too. It may look complicated, but just follow the recipe step-by-step...it will come together like magic!

6 2-oz. sqs. white melting
   chocolate, divided
1-1/2 c. pretzel sticks
few drops orange food coloring
2 c. graham cereal squares

3/4 c. Halloween-colored
   candy-coated chocolates
3/4 c. mini marshmallows
1/2 c. chocolate sprinkles

Place 1-1/2 squares white chocolate in a small microwave-safe bowl. Microwave, uncovered, on medium setting for one minute; stir. Repeat as necessary, stirring every 15 seconds, until completely melted. Place pretzel sticks in a medium bowl. Pour in melted white chocolate and stir until all pieces arc coated. Spread pretzel sticks onto wax paper, separating pieces; let stand until set. Place remaining white chocolate in a medium microwave-safe bowl. Microwave, uncovered, on medium setting for one minute; stir. Repeat, stirring every 15 seconds, until completely melted. Stir in food coloring until white chocolate is tinted bright orange. Place cereal in a large bowl. Pour in half of orange-tinted chocolate and stir until cereal is evenly coated. Add candies, marshmallows and sprinkles to cereal. Pour in remaining orange-tinted chocolate; stir until mix is evenly coated. Stir in coated pretzel sticks. Break mix into small clusters and spread out on wax paper; let set before serving. Store in an airtight container. Makes 5 cups.

Show your spirit...dress up a garden scarecrow in a hometown football jersey. Go team!

Speedy Sausage Scoops

Rebecca Etling
Blairsville, PA

*Crunchy, cheesy, yummy finger food! This is one of my favorite
quickie appetizers when I need something fast. You can use
hot sausage if you like your snacks a bit spicier.*

1 lb. ground pork sausage,
  browned and drained
8-oz. pkg. cream cheese,
  softened

10-1/2 oz. pkg. scoop-type
  corn chips
1 c. shredded Cheddar cheese

Place sausage and cream cheese in a bowl; mix until well blended.
Spoon mixture into corn chip scoops; sprinkle with shredded cheese.
Place chips on a microwave-safe plate. Microwave for 30 seconds, or
until cheese is melted. Serve immediately. Serves 6 to 8.

    I came up with this idea one year for Thanksgiving. Everyone
loved it! Get two large real or artificial pumpkins and a selection
of permanent markers in brown, orange and maroon or
other dark colors. Decorate one pumpkin by drawing fall leaves
and vines. Add a favorite Thanksgiving Bible verse. On the
other pumpkin, write "We are thankful for..." Display the
pumpkins and markers near your entryway. As your guests
arrive, invite them to write what they're thankful for on the
second pumpkin. I predict your guests will enjoy this
as much as mine did.

-Michelle Caldwell, Totz, KY

Soups, Sides & Salads

Cranberry-Apple Sweet Potatoes

Terri Melton
Taft, CA

This sweet, fruity dish is a must at our family dinner gathering every Thanksgiving. Enjoy!

21-oz. can apple pie filling
2 18-oz. cans sweet potatoes, drained and cut into bite-size pieces

8-oz. can whole-berry cranberry sauce
2 T. apricot preserves
2 T. orange marmalade

Spread pie filling in a lightly greased 8"x8" baking pan. Arrange sweet potatoes on top. Mix remaining ingredients; spoon over sweet potatoes. Bake, uncovered, at 350 degrees for 20 to 25 minutes, until hot and bubbly. Serves 6.

When I was a young girl, my mother and I always got together with Grandma and Great-Grandma for the fall harvest. This included shucking corn, canning vegetables, making relishes, apple butter and apple cider and doing other things to prepare for winter. It was believed that all should get together to help one another out. As a small child, this seemed like such a waste of time to me...after all, there were much more important things to be doing, like crunching leaves or playing with the dog. But now this is a very fond memory of mine...how often does one have four generations of loved ones helping one another out? It taught me to always treasure the time we spend with our family. Even the most everyday activities can become cherished memories if we look at them in the right way.

Wendy Love, Hillsboro, OR

Sweet Potato Toss

Janet Monnett
Cloverdale, IN

As my family and I were changing to a vegetarian diet, I tried to create dishes that everyone would find tasty. This is a delicious side dish that we all just love!

canola oil for frying
2 sweet potatoes, peeled and
   sliced
4 potatoes, peeled and sliced

1/2 to 1 T. onion powder
1/8 t. sugar
salt to taste

Into a skillet over medium-high heat, add oil to 1/2-inch depth. Combine all potato slices in a bowl; toss with seasonings. Add potatoes to hot oil in skillet. Cover and cook, turning as needed. Reduce heat to medium when potatoes begin to soften. Uncover for the last 3 to 4 minutes of cooking to crisp up potatoes. Serves 4 to 6.

To create a fragrant pumpkin, use an apple corer to carve out round vents in a hollowed-out pumpkin. Rub pumpkin pie spice on the underside of the pumpkin's lid or push whole cloves into it. Set a lighted tealight candle inside. This will give off a delightful scent for about six hours.

Cranberry Gelatin Salad

Sarah Oravecz
Gooseberry Patch

I made this the first time I was asked to bring a cranberry dish to my boyfriend's family Thanksgiving dinner. I was a little nervous how it would turn out...but it was delicious! Since then, I've made it for several more Thanksgiving dinners.

2 3-oz. pkgs. raspberry gelatin
  mix
3 c. boiling water
16-oz. can whole-berry
  cranberry sauce
20-oz. can crushed pineapple

8-oz. pkg. cream cheese,
  softened
8-oz. container sour cream
1/4 c. sugar
1 c. chopped pecans

Dissolve gelatin mix in boiling water. Add cranberry sauce and undrained pineapple; mix well. Pour half of of gelatin mixture into a 13"x9" glass baking pan; cover and refrigerate for one hour. Cover remaining gelatin mixture; let stand at room temperature. In a separate bowl, blend remaining ingredients. Spread cream cheese mixture over chilled, set gelatin layer. Return to refrigerator for about 10 minutes; pour remaining gelatin mixture over top of cream cheese layer. Refrigerate for 3 to 4 hours, until firm. Cut into squares. Makes 20 servings.

On warm fall days, set up harvest tables and chairs outdoors for a soup supper. Decorate with plump pumpkins, bittersweet wreaths, straw bales and scarecrows. End the day with a hayride in the country.

Strawberry-Cranberry Salad

Charlotte Smith
Tyrone, PA

We serve this salad for just about every holiday year 'round...it's so good you can enjoy it anytime! It needs to chill for quite awhile, so be sure to start a day ahead.

2 3-oz. pkgs. strawberry gelatin mix
2 c. boiling water
20-oz. can crushed pineapple, drained and 1/2 c. juice reserved
16-oz. can whole-berry cranberry sauce
10-oz. pkg. frozen sliced strawberries, thawed
1 c. chopped walnuts

In a large bowl, mix together gelatin mix and boiling water; stir until dissolved. Add remaining ingredients; mix well. Cover and chill for 12 to 24 hours. Transfer to a serving bowl; stir before serving. Serves 20.

Make a mini recipe album for a tried & true friend. Jot down favorite recipes on individual cards, along with your special touches or hints for success. Slip the cards into the pages of a mini photo album and tie with a homespun ribbon. Add a handwritten note that says, "I'm thankful we're friends." She'll think of you whenever she uses it!

Country-Style Creamed Cabbage

Candra Graves
Mannford, OK

For as long as I can remember, this old-fashioned recipe has been served at Thanksgiving and Christmas. We love it!

10 c. cabbage, chopped
Optional: 1/4 c. bacon drippings
10-3/4 oz. can cream of chicken
  soup

1/4 c. milk
8-oz. pkg. pasteurized process
  cheese spread, cubed
salt and pepper to taste

Place cabbage and bacon drippings, if using, in a large stockpot. Add enough water to cover. Boil over medium-high heat until tender, about 45 minutes to one hour, adding more water if needed. While cabbage is cooking, mix together remaining ingredients in a large bowl. Drain cabbage and add to soup mixture; mix well. Place in a greased 13"x9" baking pan. Bake, uncovered, at 350 degrees for 30 minutes, until bubbly and cheese has melted. Serves 8.

When the weather starts to turn chilly, sort through your family's closets and donate gently used and outgrown coats, clothes and extra blankets to a nearby charity. They'll be much appreciated!

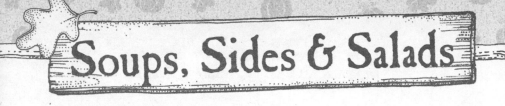

Italian Zucchini

Kari Mott
Galloway, OH

A tasty way to use up some of those end-of-the-season zucchini from the garden.

1/4 c. olive oil
1 onion, thinly sliced
14-1/2 oz. can diced tomatoes
2 to 3 zucchini, sliced

1 T. Italian seasoning
1 t. salt
Garnish: 1/4 c. grated Parmesan
   cheese

Heat oil in a skillet over medium heat. Stir in onion and cook until tender. Mix in tomatoes with juice, zucchini, Italian seasoning and salt. Cook and stir until zucchini is tender, about 5 to 10 minutes. Garnish with Parmesan cheese. Serves 4.

When the kids are studying another country in school, why not try out a food from that country? Let them help choose a recipe and shop for the ingredients...you'll all learn so much together and have fun doing it!

Chill-Chaser Noodle Soup

Sherry Shuford
Lynchburg, VA

Every year we head out to our local pumpkin patch for some fall family fun. Afterwards, everyone is tired and hungry from picking pumpkins, walking the corn maze and going on a hayride. This satisfying soup is quick & easy. I serve it with homemade popovers.

1/2 onion, chopped
2 stalks celery, chopped
2 to 3 t. oil
2 14-1/2 oz. cans chicken broth
1/4 c. roasted red peppers, drained
15-oz. can mixed vegetables
3 boneless, skinless chicken breasts, cooked and diced
1 t. poultry seasoning
1 t. garlic powder
16-oz. pkg. thin egg noodles, uncooked

In a large stockpot over medium heat, sauté onion and celery in oil until translucent. Add remaining ingredients except noodles. Reduce heat and simmer, uncovered, for 25 to 30 minutes. Stir in noodles. Simmer an additional 10 to 15 minutes, until noodles are tender. Makes 8 servings.

Dot's Popovers

Nadine Jones
Corinth, ME

It was always a treat when Gram made her popovers. They are especially good with a hot bowl of chili or stew. Gram always cautioned me not to open the oven while they were baking.

2 eggs, beaten
1 c. milk
1 c. all-purpose flour
1/2 t. salt

Mix all ingredients together thoroughly. Pour into well-greased muffin cups, filling 3/4 full. Place muffin tin in a cold oven; set temperature to 450 degrees. Bake for 30 minutes without opening oven door. Makes 6 to 8.

Soups, Sides & Salads

Trick-or-Treaters' Taco Soup

Olivia Gust
Independence, OR

*We always make this quick, yummy soup for Halloween dinner
before trick-or-treating. It keeps our tummies warm as we're
out & about visiting family & friends.*

1 lb. ground beef
1/2 c. onion, chopped
14-1/2 oz. can diced tomatoes
15-1/4 oz. can corn
16-oz. can kidney beans
15-oz. can tomato sauce

1-1/4 oz. pkg. taco seasoning
  mix
Garnish: shredded Cheddar
  cheese, sour cream, sliced
  olives, corn chips

In a large stockpot over medium heat, brown beef and onion. Drain;
stir in undrained vegetables, tomato sauce and seasoning mix.
Simmer, uncovered, for 20 minutes, stirring often. Garnish bowls of
soup as desired. Serves 6.

Cowboy Biscuits

Sheila Connolly-Mainous
Valrico, FL

*My mother interpreted this recipe from my father's description. The
biscuits were made in the cow camps where my dad spent the winter.
She said it was quite a challenge...the cowboys didn't use cups or
spoons for measuring, they used tin cans and their hands!*

2 c. all-purpose flour
1 T. baking powder
3/4 t. salt

1 c. milk
3 T. shortening or bacon
  drippings, melted

In a bowl, mix flour, baking powder and salt thoroughly. Make a well
in the center; pour in milk and shortening or drippings. Stir just until
moistened. Turn dough out onto a floured surface; turn over and pat
to about 1/2 inch thick. Use a biscuit cutter to cut, or just cut into
squares to save time. Place biscuits on a greased baking sheet. Bake
at 425 degrees for about 15 minutes, until golden. Makes 8.

Champagne Fruit Salad

Elizabeth Burkhalter
Oshkosh, WI

I have fond memories of my grandma making this fruit dish every Thanksgiving and Christmas. It's sweet and almost tastes like dessert, but we usually serve it as a side dish along with the turkey and all the trimmings. It got its name because it could be served with a glass of champagne!

8-oz. pkg. cream cheese,
  softened
3/4 c. sugar
10-oz. pkg. frozen sliced
  strawberries, thawed and
  drained
2 bananas, sliced

8-oz. can crushed pineapple,
  drained
1 c. chopped pecans
1 c. sweetened flaked coconut
10-oz. container frozen whipped
  topping, thawed

In a large bowl, blend together cream cheese and sugar with an electric mixer on medium speed. Stir in remaining ingredients by hand. Spread in a 13"x9" baking pan. Cover and freeze until firm, 3 to 4 hours. Remove from freezer a few minutes before serving time; cut into squares. Serves 12.

Scatter pressed autumn leaves on a crisp white tablecloth for a simple and splendid decoration. Layer leaves between paper towels, then between sections of newspaper. Top with a heavy book or other weight...leaves will be ready in a week or two. If time is short, you can substitute silk leaves from the craft store.

Cranberry-Orange Sauce

Ashley Billings
Norfolk, VA

This is a flavorful twist on classic cranberry sauce...it's a Thanksgiving favorite at my house!

16-oz. pkg. fresh cranberries   1/2 c. sugar
1 c. orange juice

Combine all ingredients in a stockpot over medium heat. Simmer, stirring occasionally, until cranberries begin to burst and sauce thickens, about 15 minutes. Let cool; serve at room temperature. Serves 8.

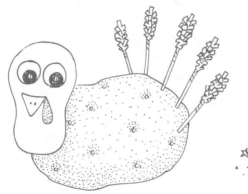

My three girls and I used to make "potato turkeys" while Thanksgiving dinner was cooking. It kept them busy while waiting and the turkeys were so cute on the dining table. Choose a potato with a flat bottom, so it will sit and not roll. Cut out a turkey head shape from construction paper and draw on a face. Glue the head to a plain toothpick and poke it into the front of the potato. For the turkey's tailfeathers, poke some frilled cocktail toothpicks into the back of the potato. You now have a little potato turkey to place on your Thanksgiving table. My girls would keep their turkeys well after the holiday, until the potatoes grew sprouts!

-Marcia Bills, Orleans, NE

Cheesy Corn & Hominy Posole

Paul Shoup
Caseville, MI

A meatless Mexican dish that feeds an army! Our yummy version came from the border town of El Paso, Texas.

1 onion, chopped
2 4-oz. cans chopped green
   chiles
10-3/4 oz. can cream of
   mushroom soup

3 c. shredded Cheddar cheese
2 15-1/2 oz. cans hominy,
   drained
2 15-oz. cans shoepeg corn,
   drained

Combine onion, chiles, soup and cheese in a large bowl. Add hominy and corn; mix well. Transfer to a 13"x9" baking pan sprayed with non-stick vegetable spray. Cover with aluminum foil. Place a pan of water on the rack beneath pan in oven. Bake at 350 degrees for 30 minutes, or until heated through and cheese is melted. Serves 6 to 8.

Hard-skinned winter squash is versatile, tasty and cooks in a jiffy in the microwave. Place a halved, seeded squash cut-side down in a microwave-safe dish. Microwave on high until tender and easily pierced. Acorn squash will take about 6 to 8 minutes, butternut squash about 10 to 13 minutes. After cooking, the squash pulp can be scooped out and mixed with butter, spices and other ingredients.

Quick & Easy Pinto Beans

Pam Massey
Marshall, AR

A terrific meal on a cold day! Brown the meat and onion ahead of time, then just add the canned ingredients for a very fast supper. A great dish for nights when Dad is doing the cooking!

1 lb. ground beef or turkey
1 onion, diced
2 10-oz. cans diced tomatoes
   with green chiles

2 16-oz. cans pinto beans
Garnish: tortilla chips, shredded
   Cheddar cheese, sour cream

Brown meat and onion together in a skillet over medium heat; drain. Add undrained tomatoes with chiles; bring to a boil. Stir in undrained beans. Simmer for 15 minutes, stirring often. Serve with tortilla chips and desired toppings. Serves 8.

A muffin tin is useful when you're serving tacos, enchiladas, chili or bean soup with lots of tasty toppings.
Fill up the sections with shredded cheese, tortilla chips, guacamole, diced tomatoes and sour cream...and let everyone mix & match their favorites!

Game-Day BBQ Onions

Cheryl Breeden
North Platte, NE

*So simple...a true football night party favorite that will
turn anyone into an onion lover!*

11-oz. pkg. mesquite barbecue-
   flavored potato chips, divided
2 10-3/4 oz. cans cream of
   chicken soup
1/2 c. milk

4 sweet onions, thinly sliced
   and divided
2 c. shredded sharp Cheddar
   cheese, divided

Crush 2 cups of potato chips; set aside. Whisk together soups and milk;
set aside. Place half of onion slices in the bottom of a 13"x9" baking
pan coated with non-stick vegetable spray. Spread uncrushed chips
over onions; add one cup cheese and half of soup mixture. Repeat
layering. Top with reserved crushed chips. Bake, uncovered, at
350 degrees for one hour. Serves 10.

Host a tailgating cook-off. Invite everyone in the neighborhood
to bring their own game-day specialty like chili, chicken wings
or barbecued ribs. You provide the beverages, baskets of warm
cornbread and plenty of napkins. Have a prize for the winner!

Swiss-Onion Casserole

Dolores McCurry
Pueblo, CO

*My mother-in-law gave me this recipe many years ago. It's always
a big hit when I take it to church suppers and other events...a delicious
side dish that goes with just about anything.*

6 onions, sliced
1/2 c. plus 3 T. butter, softened
   and divided
10-oz. pkg. shredded Swiss
   cheese
10-3/4 oz. can cream of
   mushroom with roasted
   garlic soup

1/2 c. milk
1 t. soy sauce
pepper to taste
12 to 15 slices baguette bread,
   sliced 1/2-inch thick

In a skillet over medium heat, sauté onions in 2 to 3 tablespoons
butter until tender. Spread in a lightly greased 13"x9" baking pan.
Cover with cheese; set aside. In a saucepan over medium heat, stir
together soup, milk, soy sauce and pepper. Heat until bubbly; spoon
over cheese. Spread remaining butter over both sides of bread.
Arrange bread on top of casserole. Bake, uncovered, at 350 degrees
for 30 minutes. Serves 10.

Whip up cozy throws in bright red or russet plaid fleece...simply
snip fringe all around the edges. They're so easy, you can make
one for each member of the family in no time at all.

Autumn Acorn Squash

Jenny Sarbacker
Madison, WI

*A family fall favorite! This recipe started with one my mom
used to make for us...I've added a few touches of my own.*

2 acorn squash, halved and
   seeded
2 apples, peeled, cored and
   chopped
3 T. brown sugar, packed

3 T. chopped pecans
1 t. all-purpose flour
1/4 t. cinnamon
2 T. butter, softened

Place acorn squash halves cut-side down in a greased 13"x9" baking
pan. Bake at 350 degrees for 30 minutes. Combine remaining
ingredients. Turn squash over and fill with apple mixture. Bake,
uncovered, for another 15 to 30 minutes, until squash is soft when
pierced with a fork. Serve squash halves as is or scoop contents into
a serving bowl. Serves 4.

Jumping in leaf piles is a not-to-be-missed part of childhood
fun! No fallen leaves in your yard? Ask some neighbors
with a big maple tree or two for permission to
rake up their leaves...you'll have a ball!

Soups, Sides & Salads

String Beans & Corn Casserole

Donna Clement
Picayune, MS

Whenever our family gets together, someone always asks,
"Who's making the string bean casserole?"

2 14-1/2 oz. cans French-cut green beans, drained
2 15-oz. cans shoepeg corn, drained
1/4 c. onion, chopped
1/4 c. celery, chopped
8-oz. container sour cream
10-3/4 oz. can cream of celery soup
4-1/2 oz. pkg. cheese crackers, crushed
1/4 c. margarine, melted
Garnish: slivered almonds

In a bowl, mix vegetables, sour cream and soup. Place in a lightly greased 13"x9" baking pan. Mix crushed crackers and melted margarine; sprinkle over casserole, followed by almonds. Bake, uncovered, at 375 degrees for 30 minutes, or until hot and bubbly. Makes 8 to 12 servings.

Always keep the pantry stocked with canned vegetables, hearty soups, rice and pasta for quick-to-make side dishes.

Savory Pumpkin Soup

Sarah Cameron
Maryville, TN

A scrumptious beginning to any autumn meal. Garnish with a swirl of cream and a toss of toasted pumpkin seeds.

1/2 c. onion, finely chopped
2 T. butter
1 T. all-purpose flour
2 14-oz. cans chicken broth
15-oz. can pumpkin

1 t. brown sugar, packed
1/4 t. salt
1/8 t. pepper
1/8 t. nutmeg
1 c. whipping cream

In a large saucepan over medium heat, sauté onion in butter until tender. Gradually stir in remaining ingredients except cream; bring to a boil. Reduce heat; simmer for 5 minutes. Stir in cream and simmer for about 2 minutes, until heated through. Serves 4.

Just for fun, use a hollowed-out pumpkin as a soup tureen, but try something unexpected. An all-white Lumina pumpkin or a plump green and orange Cinderella pumpkin makes the prettiest presentation!

Chicken & Barley Soup

Angela Murphy
Tempe, AZ

We like to substitute leftover turkey from Thanksgiving dinner in this hearty, quick & easy soup. It's a terrific pick-me-up after a day of post-Thanksgiving shopping.

1 c. onion, chopped
1 c. carrot, peeled and chopped
1/2 c. celery, chopped
2 cloves garlic, minced
2 t. olive oil
2 14-1/2 oz. cans chicken broth

1/2 c. quick-cooking barley, uncooked
1-3/4 c. water
1/4 t. salt
1/4 t. pepper
1 c. cooked chicken, cubed

In a Dutch oven over medium-high heat, sauté onion, carrot, celery and garlic in oil for 5 minutes, until onion is tender. Add broth, barley, water and seasonings. Bring to a boil; reduce heat and simmer, partially covered, about 25 minutes, until vegetables are tender. Add chicken; heat through. Serves 4.

toasty

When my daughter was little, I began making Pumpkin Stew, which is simmered on the stove, ladled into a hollowed-out pumpkin and placed into the oven to finish cooking. When it is served, you scoop out the pumpkin along with the stew. This was always our dinner the night before Halloween and it became a tradition. My daughter is married now with two little girls of her own, and they still come to my house to share Pumpkin Stew. I set the table in fall colors, with torn muslin for napkins, plastic spiders for napkin rings and Halloween crackers to pop open. It's my favorite time of year...we all look forward to it!

-Connie Peterson, Sunland, CA

Mom's Butternut Squash Bake

Sue Ellen Crabb
Glendale, AZ

My mom got this recipe in a cooking class she took. I remember how delicious it was with fresh veggies from our garden! She made it every Thanksgiving until she passed away, then it became my turn.

10-3/4 oz. can cream of chicken
  soup
1 c. sour cream
1 c. carrots, peeled and
  shredded
2 lbs. butternut squash, cooked
  and lightly mashed

1/4 c. onion, chopped
8-oz. pkg. herb-flavored stuffing
  mix
1/2 c. butter, melted

In a bowl, combine soup and sour cream; stir in carrots. Fold in squash and onion. Combine stuffing mix and butter; spread 1/2 of mixture in bottom of a lightly greased 3-quart casserole dish. Spoon in squash mixture. Top with remaining stuffing mix. Bake, uncovered, at 350 degrees for 25 to 30 minutes. Serves 6 to 8.

To poke a wood fire is more solid enjoyment
than almost anything else in the world.

-Charles Dudley Warner

Icebox Mashed Potatoes

Helen Helgeson
Albany, OR

*These delicious potatoes are a real time-saver! They can be made ahead
of time and kept refrigerated for several days. I make this for our
church's Thanksgiving feast...everyone likes them!*

5 lbs. potatoes, peeled and quartered	2 t. onion salt
1 c. sour cream	1 t. salt
3/4 c. cream cheese, softened	1/4 t. pepper
2 T. butter, softened	Garnish: additional butter, sliced

In a stockpot over medium-high heat, cook potatoes in boiling salted
water until tender, about 20 minutes. Drain; mash until smooth. Add
remaining ingredients except garnish. Beat until light and fluffy. Cool;
cover and refrigerate up to 3 days. To serve, place desired amount of
potatoes in a well-buttered casserole dish. Dot with butter. Bake,
uncovered, at 350 degrees until heated through, about 20 to
30 minutes. Potatoes may also be reheated in the microwave.
Makes 15 to 20 servings.

When topping a casserole with bread crumbs, potato chips or
cereal, place in a plastic zipping bag and seal. Roll with a heavy
rolling pin until the crumbs are crushed...clean-up is a breeze!

Pear Harvest Salad

Lori Ritchey
Narvon, PA

I love a sweet, crunchy salad with fruit and nuts. This is a delicious combination that's just right for any autumn meal.

8-oz. pkg. mixed salad greens
15-oz. can pear halves, drained
   and 1/3 c. juice reserved
1/2 c. chopped walnuts or
   pecans, toasted

1/4 red onion, thinly sliced and
   separated into rings
2/3 c. blue cheese salad
   dressing

Place salad greens in a large salad bowl. Top with pear halves, nuts and onion. Stir reserved pear juice into salad dressing; drizzle over salad. Serve immediately. Serves 6 to 8.

Banana Bread

Julie Latendresse
Quebec, Canada

A friend gave me this easy recipe.

1-1/2 c. all-purpose flour
1 c. brown sugar, packed
1 t. baking soda
1/2 t. salt

3 bananas, mashed
1/2 c. mayonnaise
1 egg, beaten
1/2 c. chopped nuts

In a bowl, mix together flour, brown sugar, baking soda and salt; set aside. In a separate bowl, blend together bananas, mayonnaise and egg. Add flour mixture to banana mixture. Mix gently just until moistened; stir in nuts. Pour batter into a greased 8"x4" loaf pan. Place pan on center rack of oven. Bake at 350 degrees for one hour. Cool completely before slicing. Makes one loaf.

A crock of honey butter...so yummy on warm bread, biscuits and muffins. Simply blend together 1/2 cup each of honey and softened butter.

Tart Apple Salad

Leona Krivda
Belle Vernon, PA

*My husband really likes this nice fall salad. I always
serve it at Thanksgiving.*

6 tart crisp apples, peeled, cored
    and chopped
1-1/2 c. red grapes, halved
    and seeded
1 c. celery, finely chopped
1/2 c. chopped walnuts
1/4 c. sugar

1 T. mayonnaise-style salad
    dressing
1/2 pt. whipping cream,
    whipped
1/4 c. sweetened dried
    cranberries

Toss together apples, grapes, celery and walnuts in a large serving
bowl; sprinkle with sugar. Stir in salad dressing; mix well. Cover and
chill until serving time. Fold in whipped cream and cranberries just
before serving. Serves 10 to 12.

The simplest table decorations are often the most charming!
Fill a rustic wooden bowl with shiny red apples or fragrant
yellow lemons for the kitchen table, or pile the bowl with
bright-colored balls of yarn for a crafting corner.

Cream Cheesy Mexican Corn

Anne Welborn
Fort Wayne, IN

This recipe brings memories of a time when I worked as a university resident director. When the students went home for Thanksgiving, several of us resident directors would stay to supervise those who remained on campus. The dean of residence life invited me to his family's home for Thanksgiving dinner so I would not have to spend it alone. This is the dish I took...it was a hit!

2 15-oz. cans corn, drained
1/2 green pepper, diced

1/2 red pepper, diced
8-oz. pkg. cream cheese, cubed

Combine all ingredients in a saucepan over medium-low heat. Cook, stirring occasionally, until cream cheese melts and peppers are cooked through. Serves 6.

Greet your guests with a whimsical pumpkin tower on the front porch. Arrange pumpkins and squash in graduated sizes in a stack, using skewers to hold them in place. Clever!

Corn Mazatlán

Tracee Cummins
Amarillo, TX

This recipe originally came from the label on a can of corn. I've tweaked it slightly over the years to suit my family's tastes, and it's one of our favorites. It's easy, fast and tastes like you worked all day, but you don't even have to turn the oven on!

16-oz. can corn, drained and
   1/4 cup liquid reserved
16-oz. can shoepeg corn,
   drained
1/4 c. green pepper, chopped
1/4 c. green onions, chopped

2 4-oz. cans chopped green
   chiles
1 t. ground cumin
8-oz. pkg. cream cheese,
   softened

In a saucepan over low heat, combine reserved corn liquid and cream cheese. Cook and stir until smooth. Stir in remaining ingredients and heat through. Serves 8 to 10.

A no-fuss side...tuck some roasted vegetables into the oven along with a main-dish casserole. Toss peeled, sliced veggies with olive oil and spread on a baking sheet. Bake at 350 degrees, stirring occasionally, for about 30 minutes, until tender. Sweet potatoes, beets, leeks and Brussels sprouts are all tasty...choose a favorite or mix 'em up!

Mom's Filling Balls

Beth Myers
Dover, PA

I remember Mom making these filling balls for all the holidays. My grandma used to cut up the celery, and when she passed away, it became my job. Try this recipe...I think you'll love it!

15-oz. pkg. stuffing cubes
1 T. dried parsley
pepper to taste
1/2 c. onion, chopped
1/2 c. celery, chopped

1/2 c. margarine
2 cubes chicken bouillon
1 c. boiling water
2 eggs, beaten
1/3 c. milk

Place stuffing cubes in a large bowl; sprinkle with parsley and pepper and set aside. In a skillet over medium heat, sauté onion and celery in margarine until tender. Dissolve bouillon in boiling water; add to onion mixture. Remove from heat; pour over stuffing mixture. In a separate bowl, stir together eggs and milk. Pour over stuffing mixture; toss to mix well. Form into 6 to 8 balls; place on a greased baking sheet. Bake, uncovered, at 325 degrees for 25 to 30 minutes. Serves 6 to 8.

Dressing, stuffing or filling...whatever you call it, it's better with gravy! Measure 1/4 cup pan drippings from your turkey or beef roast into a skillet over medium heat. Stir in 1/4 cup flour. Cook and stir until smooth and bubbly. Add 2 cups skimmed pan juices or broth; cook and stir until boiling. Boil for about one minute, to desired thickness. Add salt and pepper to taste.

Grandmother's Scalloped Oysters
Kay Neubauer
Taylorsville, NC

My grandmother always served this dish at Thanksgiving and Christmas. When my son-in-law joined our family, it quickly became a favorite of his too. This casserole reheats well in the microwave.

1/2 c. round buttery crackers, crumbled
1/2 c. saltine crackers, crumbled
1 pt. fresh oysters, drained and liquid reserved

1/2 t. pepper, divided
1/2 c. butter, sliced and divided
1 to 1-1/2 c. whipping cream

Mix cracker crumbs together. Place 1/3 of crumbs in a buttered shallow 1-1/2 quart casserole dish. Spread half of oysters over crumbs; sprinkle with half of pepper and dot with half of butter. Make a second layer; top with remaining cracker crumbs. Combine reserved oyster liquid and cream; pour over casserole. With a knife, make slits all over the top so the liquid will go all through the dish. Bake, uncovered, at 400 degrees for 25 to 30 minutes, until heated through and golden on top. Serves 8.

Purchase a bundle of wheat straw at a craft store. Arrange a few stalks on each folded napkin for a beautiful yet simple reminder of a bountiful harvest.

Joan's Ratatoûille

Joan Shaffer
Chambersburg, PA

I created this recipe from the abundant supply of fresh vegetables my father grows every year. He so enjoys sharing his garden bounty with family & friends! This is a delicious side dish, but I enjoy serving it in rimmed soup plates as soup.

2 c. onion, chopped
4 cloves garlic, minced
1/2 c. olive oil
8 c. tomatoes, peeled and
   coarsely chopped
4 to 6 c. zucchini, cut into
   1/2-inch thick slices

2 green peppers, cut into thin
   strips
2 red peppers, cut into thin
   strips
1 T. chili powder, or to taste
salt to taste

In a large saucepan over medium heat, sauté onion and garlic in oil, about 3 to 4 minutes. Add tomatoes, zucchini and peppers. Reduce heat; cover and simmer, stirring occasionally, until vegetables are tender, about 20 minutes. Stir in seasonings. Simmer, uncovered, an additional 15 minutes, stirring occasionally. Serves 6.

Visit the farmers' market for the best homegrown veggies...toss a market basket in the car and let the kids pick out fresh flavors for tonight's dinner.

Cheesy Veggie Soup

Jenny Bishoff
Mount Lake Park, MD

My grandmother makes this simple, satisfying soup for my girls & me after a busy day of work and school. Really good!

1 to 2 14-oz. cans chicken
  broth
16-oz. pkg. frozen California-
  blend vegetables

1 lb. pasteurized process cheese
  spread, cubed
Garnish: croutons or crackers

Place broth and vegetables in a large saucepan. Cover and cook according to directions on vegetable package; do not drain. When tender, mash vegetables with a potato masher; stir in cheese. Stir gently over low heat until cheese is melted and soup is heated through. Serve with croutons or crackers. Serves 4 to 6.

Autumn is a terrific time to get outdoors. Place a hook
by the back door and keep a favorite comfy sweater on it.
You never know when you'll want to run outside to see the
colorful trees or a harvest moon.

Mashed Root Vegetables

Mary Lou Thomas
Portland, ME

This side dish is so delicious I often forget to eat whatever else is on my plate. And it's such a great way to use autumn veggies!

1/2 lb. sweet potatoes, peeled and cubed
1/2 lb. parsnips, peeled and cubed
1/2 lb. celery root, peeled and cubed

2 to 3 T. olive oil
salt and pepper to taste
1 lb. potatoes, peeled and cubed
3 T. butter, softened
1/2 c. milk

In a bowl, toss together sweet potatoes, parsnips and celery root with oil, salt and pepper. Place on an ungreased 15"x10" jelly-roll pan. Bake at 350 degrees for 20 to 25 minutes, until golden. Meanwhile, place potatoes in a large saucepan and cover with salted water. Bring to a boil over medium-high heat; reduce heat to medium and cook until tender, about 12 to 15 minutes. Drain; return potatoes to the pot. Add roasted vegetables and butter; mash and stir until butter melts. Add milk; stir to mix. Season to taste with additional salt and pepper. Serves 6.

Roast garlic is heavenly to spread on bread and so easy in the microwave! Slice the top off a whole garlic bulb and set it in a microwave-safe container. Sprinkle to taste with salt, pepper and olive oil, add a little water and cover with plastic wrap. Microwave on high for about 8 minutes, until soft.

Herbed Mashed Potatoes   *Vickie*

Filled with fresh herbs, these potatoes are just wonderful!
Serve topped with a large melting pat of butter, of course.

6-1/2 c. potatoes, peeled and
    cubed
2 cloves garlic, halved
1/2 c. milk
1/2 c. sour cream
1 T. butter, softened

2 T. fresh parsley, minced
2 T. fresh oregano, minced
1 T. fresh thyme, minced
3/4 t. salt
1/8 t. pepper

Place potatoes and garlic in a large saucepan; add water to cover.
Bring to a boil over medium-high heat. Reduce heat to medium;
simmer for 20 minutes, or until potatoes are very tender. Drain; return
potatoes and garlic to pan. Add remaining ingredients; beat with an
electric mixer on medium speed to desired consistency. Serves 6 to 8.

Make herbed butter in a jiffy to dress up mashed potatoes
or serve with warm rolls. Simply roll a stick of butter
in freshly chopped herbs, slice and serve.

Fusilli Garden Salad

Sharon Tillman
Hampton, VA

Filled with curly fusilli noodles and lots of other good stuff, this is a Halloween tradition at our house. I tell the kids that the wiggly noodles are worms...it makes them squeal, but they eat it up!

16-oz. pkg. fusilli pasta,
   uncooked and divided
1 yellow squash, halved
   lengthwise and sliced
1 c. cherry tomatoes
1 c. snow pea pods
1 c. black olives

1 c. green olives with pimentos
4 green onions, thinly sliced
1 c. Cheddar cheese, diced
1 c. sliced almonds, toasted
8-oz. bottle Italian salad
   dressing

Divide pasta in half, reserving the remainder for a future use. Cook remaining pasta according to package directions; drain and rinse with cold water. In a large bowl, combine cooked pasta and remaining ingredients except salad dressing. Add desired amount of salad dressing; toss gently to coat. Cover and chill at least 2 hours before serving. Serves 12.

Turn a bowl of cream soup into spiderweb soup...eek! Spoon several tablespoons of sour cream into a plastic zipping bag. Snip off one corner and squeeze the sour cream in circles on the soup. To create a web effect, pull a toothpick across the circles, from the center to the edges. Fun for Halloween!

Mom's Cucumber Gelatin Salad
Natasha Morris
Lamar, CO

This cool, refreshing salad is always requested for our family's holiday dinners...it's terrific with roast turkey.

3-oz. pkg. lime gelatin mix
1 t. salt
1 c. boiling water
2 T. vinegar
1 t. onion, grated

1/8 t. pepper
1 c. sour cream
1/2 c. mayonnaise
2 c. cucumbers, peeled and
    diced

Combine gelatin mix and salt with boiling water; stir until dissolved. Add vinegar, onion and pepper; cover and refrigerate about one hour, until very thick. Blend in sour cream and mayonnaise; fold in cucumbers. Return to refrigerator for 3 to 4 hours, until set. Serves 10.

Drizzle spring mix greens with a quick & easy honey dressing. Whisk together 1/2 cup balsamic vinegar, 1/4 cup honey, 1/4 cup olive oil and one teaspoon soy sauce until smooth. Top salad with ruby-red pomegranate seeds or diced orange persimmons and a toss of candied pecans...yum!

Gingersnap Baked Beans

Nancy Elder
Lincoln, NE

I found this easy recipe years ago in a women's magazine...the gingersnaps add a flavor that's just a little different! This hearty dish has become one of our favorites for cookouts.

4 slices bacon, crisply cooked
   and crumbled
2 16-oz. cans pork & beans
2 T. onion, chopped

1/4 c. brown sugar, packed
1/4 c. catsup
3/4 c. gingersnap cookies,
   crushed

In a large bowl, mix together all ingredients. Spoon into a greased 1-1/2 quart casserole dish. Bake, uncovered, at 375 degrees for 30 minutes, or until hot and bubbly. Serves 6 to 8.

Casseroles that feed a crowd are great take-alongs for any harvest party. Keep them warm by wrapping the dish in aluminum foil and then tucking into a newspaper-lined basket.

Honey-Mustard Sweet Potatoes

Tara Horton
Gooseberry Patch

Being a mustard fanatic, I enjoy working it into all kinds of recipes.
These yummy potatoes are right at home on a holiday buffet.

1 T. margarine
1/2 c. onion, thinly sliced
3 sweet potatoes, peeled and cut
    into 1-inch cubes

1 c. chicken broth
1 T. Dijon mustard
1 T. honey
1/4 t. pepper

Melt margarine in a saucepan over medium heat. Sauté onion and sweet potatoes for 5 minutes. Stir in remaining ingredients; bring to a boil. Reduce heat; cover and simmer for 20 minutes, or until potatoes are tender. Remove from heat; whip with an electric mixer on medium speed until smooth. Serves 4.

I grew up in a very old house surrounded by huge maple trees. You can imagine the bounty of colorful leaves we amassed each fall! My mother taught my brothers and me to make "leaf houses" by raking small piles of leaves into long lines to form the walls of various rooms and hallways, leaving openings for the doorways. We would design huge maze-like play-homes and then we'd play for hours. I've shared this fall tradition with my own eight children and we all enjoy wandering through our leaf houses.

-Kathy White, Cato, NY

Spicy Squash Soup

Arden Regnier
East Moriches, NY

One year we were getting tired of eating leftover Thanksgiving turkey and I had a lot of leftover squash too. So I came up with this recipe...my original recipe is written on a paper napkin! It's a very satisfying supper with a basket of cornbread muffins.

2 butternut squash, peeled,
   seeded and cubed
1/2 c. brown sugar, packed
1/2 c. water
2 c. chicken broth
12-oz. can evaporated milk
1/2 onion, finely diced

1 jalapeño pepper, seeded and
   finely diced
1 stalk celery, finely diced
salt and pepper to taste
ground cumin to taste
Garnish: sour cream

Cover squash with water in a large saucepan. Cook over medium-high heat until tender; drain. Mash squash and measure out about 4 cups. Return squash to saucepan over medium-low heat; stir in remaining ingredients except cumin and sour cream. Simmer, covered, for about 45 minutes. Let cool slightly. Purée soup until smooth, using an immersion blender or adding to a blender in small batches. Return soup to saucepan just long enough to heat through; stir in cumin. Garnish servings with a dollop of sour cream. Serves 6 to 8.

Top bowls of soup with crunchy cheese toasts. Cut bread with a mini cookie cutter and brush lightly with olive oil. Place on a broiler pan and broil for 2 to 3 minutes, until golden. Turn over and sprinkle with freshly shredded Parmesan cheese. Broil another 2 to 3 minutes, until cheese melts. Yum!

Mains

Do-Ahead Roast Turkey

Marcia Rae Buehrer
Stryker, OH

My husband's aunt used to bring the roast turkey for our family's Thanksgiving gathering. She always prepared it ahead of time...perfect for carrying in and a super time-saver on Thanksgiving Day! Our church even adopted her method for its annual Harvest Dinner. This recipe can be adjusted to your favorite roasting method and any size of turkey.

10 to 12-lb. roasting turkey,   2 cubes chicken bouillon
    thawed if frozen   2 c. boiling water
salt to taste

Place turkey in an ungreased roasting pan; cover loosely with aluminum foil. Roast at 350 degrees for 2-1/2 to 3 hours. Turkey is done when a meat thermometer inserted in breast meat reads 165 degrees and the thigh reads 170 degrees. Drain off pan drippings, reserving for gravy if desired. Allow turkey to cool for about 30 minutes. Slice turkey and place in a casserole dish, keeping dark and light meat separate. Add salt to taste as the slices are layered. Dissolve bouillon cubes in boiling water; pour over turkey. Cover with aluminum foil and refrigerate for one to 2 days. Reheat, covered, at 350 degrees for 30 to 40 minutes, until warmed through. Makes 10 to 12 servings.

Thanksgiving dinner...it's all about tradition! Keep it simple with tried & true recipes everyone loves and anticipates...sweet potato casserole, corn pudding and cranberry sauce. If you like, add just one or two simple new dishes for variety. Then relax and enjoy your guests!

Mains

Turkey Crescent Squares

Beth Bundy
Long Prairie, MN

This recipe was given to me at my bridal shower. It's become my favorite turkey dish ever...yum!

3-oz. pkg. cream cheese,
   softened
3 T. butter, melted and divided
2 c. cooked turkey, cubed
2 T. milk
1 T. onion, chopped

1/8 t. salt
1/4 t. pepper
8-oz. tube refrigerated crescent
   rolls
3/4 c. seasoned croutons,
   crushed

In a large bowl, blend together cream cheese and 2 tablespoons melted butter. Add turkey, milk, onion, salt and pepper; mix well. Separate crescent rolls into 4 rectangles; firmly press perforations together. Spoon cream cheese mixture onto each rectangle. Pull up corners of dough and seal edges. Roll in remaining butter, then in crushed croutons. Place on an ungreased baking sheet. Bake, uncovered, at 350 degrees for 25 minutes, or until golden. Serves 4.

Make a trivet in a jiffy to protect the tabletop from hot dishes. Simply attach a cork or felt square to the bottom of a large ceramic tile with craft glue. It's so easy, why not make several to use on the Thanksgiving dinner table?

Thanksgiving in a Pan

Mary Patenaude
Griswold, CT

So satisfying! You can also use any leftovers you have on hand.

6-oz. pkg stuffing mix
2-1/2 c. cooked turkey, cubed
2 c. frozen green beans, thawed

12-oz. jar turkey gravy
pepper to taste

Prepare stuffing mix according to package directions. Transfer to a greased 11"x7" baking pan. Layer with remaining ingredients. Cover and bake at 350 degrees for 30 to 35 minutes, until heated through. Serves 6.

Thanksgiving is one of my favorite memories of growing up with my mother and my grandparents. Grandmother kept a beautiful set of dishes in the hall cupboard...a service for ten with dinner plates, salad plates, meat platter, gravy boat, dessert plates, teacups, sugar bowl and creamer. Every Thanksgiving Eve, she and I would take them out and wash them. It made me feel very special being allowed to help her with these dishes! When we set the table the next day, I thought we had the most elegant table anywhere. My grandmother has since passed away and the dishes are now mine, as she promised me. My mother told me that they were not expensive, but to me they were worth their weight in gold. Every time I look at the dishes, I smile about the wonderful memories we created.

-Lynne Gasier, Struthers, OH

Mains

Baked Turkey Drumstick

Phyl Broich-Wessling
Garner, IA

*Simple and fun! This recipe is easy to multiply
for more guests and clean-up is a breeze.*

1 turkey drumstick
2 slices bacon, crisply cooked
   and crumbled
2 T. oil or bacon drippings

2 T. onion, chopped
2 T. celery, chopped
1/8 t. celery salt
salt and pepper to taste

Place turkey drumstick in the center of a medium-size square of
aluminum foil. Top with remaining ingredients. Wrap foil tightly
around drumstick; place in a shallow baking pan. Bake at 400 degrees
for 1-1/2 hours, until juices run clear when drumstick is pierced.
Makes one serving.

Uh-oh...tomorrow is the big day and the turkey is still
frozen solid! Place it in a large cooler and cover with cold water,
changing the water once an hour. A 12 to 14-pound bird
will thaw in about 8 hours.

Easy Turkey Casserole

Connie Combs
Beavercreek, OH

We get tired of leftover Thanksgiving turkey, so I make lots of these casseroles in disposable baking pans and freeze them. Later, when I don't feel like cooking, I pull one out of the freezer. While it's baking, I toss together a crisp salad. We enjoy a good meal together...and I don't tell them that this is leftover Tom Turkey!

2-1/2 c. cooked turkey, shredded
4-oz. can sliced mushrooms, drained
10-3/4 oz. can cream of chicken soup
10-3/4 oz. can cream of mushroom soup
12-oz. can evaporated milk
5-oz. can chow mein noodles

Mix all ingredients together in a greased 13"x9" baking pan. Bake, uncovered, at 325 degrees for about 45 minutes, or until hot and bubbly. Serves 6 to 8.

No need to wait 'til the day after Thanksgiving to enjoy your favorite turkey casseroles! Order ready-to-use roast turkey at the supermarket deli counter for quick pantry meals. Just purchase what you need and have it sliced thick, then cube or dice to use in recipes.

Mains

After-Thanksgiving Hot Dish

Amanda Walton
Marysville, OH

One year I decided to do something new with our Thanksgiving leftovers. This was the result...and my hubby loved it! If you don't have enough leftover veggies, add a can of mixed vegetables.

4 c. chicken broth
2 c. long-cooking brown rice, uncooked
2 T. butter
1 onion, chopped
1 green pepper, chopped

3 to 4 c. cooked turkey, cubed
2 c. mixed cooked vegetables
10-3/4 oz. can cream of celery soup
salt and pepper to taste

Bring broth to a boil in a stockpot over medium heat; stir in rice. Reduce heat to low; cover and simmer for 45 minutes, or as directed on package. When rice has 15 minutes left to cook, melt butter in a skillet over medium heat. Add onion and green pepper; sauté until softened. Add turkey to skillet and heat through. When rice is done, add turkey mixture, vegetables and soup to rice. Simmer for 5 minutes, or until heated through. Add salt and pepper to taste. Serves 6 to 8.

For nifty placecard holders, simply make a small slice in seasonal whole fruits or veggies...apples, peppers or mini pumpkins. Write guests' names on cards and tuck into the slits.

Orange Turkey-Rice Dish

Shirl Parsons
Cape Carteret, NC

My son-in-law Tyler gave me this delicious recipe. It's one that he cherished as a young boy growing up in Alberta, Canada.

2-1/2 to 3 c. cooked turkey, diced
1-1/2 c. frozen orange juice concentrate, thawed

3 c. instant rice, uncooked
1 c. water
1/4 c. margarine, sliced
1/4 t. garlic, minced

Mix together all ingredients in a large microwave-safe bowl. Cover loosely with plastic wrap. Microwave on high setting for 25 minutes, or until hot and rice is tender. Fluff with a fork before serving. Serves 6.

Serve up this easy, refreshing punch at the harvest table. Scoop a quart of lemon or raspberry sherbet into 8 balls and freeze until serving time. To serve, place each ball in a frosted stemmed glass. Carefully pour 1/2 cup chilled cranberry juice cocktail over the sherbet and garnish with a sprig of fresh mint.

Mains

Penny's Turkey Enchiladas

Sandra Smith
Lancaster, CA

Penny is my pen pal in Oklahoma; we've been friends since 1965 and often exchange recipes. A few years ago, I needed a good casserole dish to serve to a houseful of out-of-town guests and she sent me this one. I doubled everything, made two of the casseroles and froze one of them for later on. It was a big hit...thanks, Penny!

8-1/2 oz. jar green enchilada
   sauce
10-3/4 oz. can cream of chicken
   soup
2 c. cooked turkey, diced
1 c. onion, diced
2 c. shredded Cheddar or
   Monterey Jack cheese,
   divided

6 to 8 corn tortillas
oil for frying
Garnish: salsa, sour cream,
   guacamole

Stir together enchilada sauce and soup in a saucepan over medium-low heat; simmer until heated through. In a separate bowl, mix together turkey, onion and one cup cheese. Pour half of sauce mixture into turkey mixture; stir well and set aside. In a skillet over medium-high heat, fry tortillas in oil, about 5 seconds each, until softened. Drain on paper towels. Spoon turkey mixture onto tortillas and roll up. Place enchiladas, seam-side down, in a 2-quart casserole dish sprayed with non-stick vegetable spray. Spoon remaining sauce mixture over top; sprinkle with remaining cheese. Bake, uncovered, at 350 degrees for 30 to 45 minutes, until hot and bubbly. Serve with desired garnishes. Serves 6 to 8.

Start a new Thanksgiving tradition...a turkey trot!
Instead of snoozing after savoring a big dinner together, lead everyone on a brisk walk. Enjoy the fresh crisp air and the last fallen leaves or the first snowflakes...you'll be ready to sample all those scrumptious pies afterwards!

Janet's Farmer's Pie

Janet Reinhart
Columbia, IL

An adaptation of a simple shepherd's pie...my children loved this when they were young. It's easy and quick, since it's made from pantry staples. I've made it numerous times for friends after a surgery or while they're moving to a new home. It's become a new favorite of our next-door neighbors who are the parents of three little kids!

13-oz. can chicken breast, drained
1/2 c. French fried onions
10-3/4 oz. can cream of chicken soup

14-1/2 oz. can green beans, drained
3 to 4 c. mashed potatoes
1/2 c. shredded Cheddar cheese

In a large bowl, combine chicken, onions, soup and beans. Transfer to an 8"x8" baking pan sprayed with non-stick vegetable spray. Spread potatoes over top. Bake, uncovered, at 350 degrees for about 20 minutes. Sprinkle cheese on top; bake an additional 10 minutes, or until bubbly around the edges and cheese melts. Makes 4 to 6 servings.

Tuck family photos into florist card holders and arrange with colorful mums...what a terrific conversation starter and table decoration for Thanksgiving dinner!

Mains

Skillet Chicken & Mushrooms

Tina Wright
Atlanta, GA

We're avid mushroom hunters! But feel free to use any kind of fresh mushrooms you like in this delicious, hearty recipe.

1-1/2 lbs. boneless, skinless
   chicken breasts
salt and pepper to taste
3 T. butter, divided
1 yellow onion, chopped

1 lb. sliced mushrooms
1/4 c. Madeira wine or chicken
   broth
1 T. Worcestershire sauce
1 T. fresh tarragon, chopped

Sprinkle chicken generously with salt and pepper. In a large skillet over medium-high heat, melt 2 tablespoons butter. Cook chicken until golden on both sides, about 8 minutes. Transfer chicken to a plate. Melt remaining butter in skillet over medium heat. Add onion; sauté just until softened, about 3 minutes. Add mushrooms; sauté until juices are released, about 5 minutes. Stir in wine or broth and Worcestershire sauce. Return chicken and any juices from the plate to the pan. Spoon mushroom mixture over chicken. Reduce heat to medium-low; cover and cook until chicken juices run clear, about 20 minutes. Stir in tarragon and additional salt and pepper, as desired. Serves 4.

Whip up lots of holiday napkin holders in a snap. Cut cardboard tubes into 2-inch lengths, then cover them with strips of shiny gold wrapping paper fastened with double-stick tape. Add a silk flower with hot glue and tuck in the napkins...gorgeous!

Simple Chicken Tetrazzini

Tonya Adams
Magnolia, KY

*One of my favorite recipes! It's delicious year 'round
and is equally good with leftover turkey.*

8-oz. pkg. spaghetti, uncooked
   and divided
2 T. butter
2 T. all-purpose flour
salt and pepper to taste
1/2 c. chicken broth

1 c. milk
2 c. cooked chicken, diced
2-oz. jar chopped pimentos,
   drained
1/4 c. shredded sharp Cheddar
   cheese

Divide pasta in half, reserving the remainder for a future use. Cook remaining pasta according to package directions; drain. Meanwhile, melt butter in a large saucepan over medium-low heat. Stir in flour, salt and pepper; blend until smooth. Add broth and milk gradually; blend well. Simmer until thickened, stirring constantly. Stir in chicken, pimentos and cooked spaghetti. Spoon into a lightly greased 2-quart casserole dish; sprinkle with cheese. Bake, uncovered, at 375 degrees for 15 to 25 minutes, until bubbly and cheese is melted. Makes 4 to 6 servings.

Hosting lots of guests for Thanksgiving dinner? Feel free to mix & match plates and glasses for a whimsical look that's more fun than carefully matched china.

Mains

Suzi's Chicken Casserole

Becky Holsinger
Reedsville, OH

My friend Suzi gave me this recipe when I got married.
It's simple to make and my husband loves it too.

2 4.3-oz. pkgs. chicken-
   flavored noodle & sauce mix
1 c. sour cream
10-3/4 oz. can cream of chicken
   soup

2 boneless, skinless chicken
   breasts, cooked and diced
6 T. butter, melted
1 sleeve round buttery crackers,
   crumbled

Prepare noodle mix according to package directions; transfer to a large
bowl. Add sour cream, soup and chicken; mix well. Spoon into a
greased 13"x9" baking pan. In a separate small bowl, pour melted
butter over crackers and toss to coat. Sprinkle over top of noodle
mixture. Bake, uncovered, at 350 degrees for about 30 minutes, or
until bubbly and golden. Serves 4.

The golden glow of candlelight adds a magic touch to any
gathering. For all the charm and none of the worry of real flames,
use battery-operated tealights in hallways, corners and other
places where they can safely be overlooked.

Chicken Biscuit Dinner

Janie Reed
Zanesville, OH

This dish just came together with ingredients I had on hand. It must have turned out well, because my husband ate enough for two!

2 boneless, skinless chicken
  breasts
1 T. oil
2 T. steak sauce
2 T. water
14-oz. can cream of mushroom
  soup

1/2 c. milk
7-oz. can sliced mushrooms,
  drained
2 T. dried, minced onion
12-oz. tube refrigerated
  buttermilk biscuits, divided
1 c. shredded Cheddar cheese

In a skillet over medium heat, cook chicken in oil until golden and juices run clear. Shred chicken and return to skillet. Add steak sauce and water; cover and simmer for 5 minutes. Add soup, milk, mushrooms and onion; continue to simmer 5 additional minutes. Slice 4 unbaked biscuits in half and use to line the bottom of a lightly greased 8"x8" baking pan. Spoon chicken mixture over biscuits. Slice remaining biscuits in half and arrange on top of chicken mixture. Bake, uncovered, at 350 degrees for 25 minutes, or until bubbly and biscuits are golden. Remove from oven; sprinkle with cheese and return to oven for 5 minutes, or until cheese is melted. Serves 4.

Make the children's table fun with special touches. Cover the table with brown kraft paper and add crayons for coloring and sugar cone "cornucopias" filled with snack mix to munch on. Kids of all sizes will beg to sit there!

Hot Chicken Salad

Gladys Kielar
Perrysburg, OH

A delicious dinner we love to share with family & friends.
It's so easy, you'll love it too!

4-lb. deli roast chicken,
  shredded
1-1/2 c. celery, chopped
1 c. mayonnaise

10-3/4 oz. can cream of chicken
  soup
1 onion, chopped
2 c. saltine crackers, crushed

Mix together all ingredients except crackers. Pour into a lightly
greased 13"x9" baking pan. Sprinkle crackers over top. Bake,
uncovered, at 375 degrees for 30 minutes, or until heated through.
Makes 4 to 6 servings.

On busy fall weekends, a simple make-ahead casserole is
perfect when you're getting together with friends. Assemble it
the day before and refrigerate, then pop it in the oven when
you return from barn sale-ing, leaf peeping or getting an
early start on holiday shopping.

Poppy Seed Chicken

*Jean Xander
Catasauqua, PA*

*Here's one of my favorite dinner recipes. It tastes
terrific...just ask my guests!*

3 boneless, skinless chicken
   breasts, cooked and cubed
8-oz. container sour cream
10-3/4 oz. can cream of chicken
   soup

1/2 c. butter, melted
1 sleeve round buttery crackers,
   crushed
2 T. poppy seed

Place chicken in a lightly greased 13"x9" baking pan. Mix together
sour cream and soup; spread over chicken. In a separate small bowl,
mix together remaining ingredients. Sprinkle on top of sour cream
mixture. Bake, uncovered, at 350 degrees for 30 minutes, or until hot
and bubbly. Makes 4 servings.

Keep the week's menu and shopping list right at your fingertips.
Criss-cross a bulletin board with tacked-on lengths of wide
rick rack and just slip lists underneath...so handy!

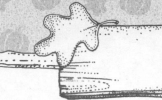

Mains

Maple-Orange Chicken

Mary Warren
Auburn, MI

My sister-in-law and I live many miles apart, but we like to exchange recipes in our conversations together. This is one she sent me that my family loves...it's very good made with pork chops also. We enjoy this with cooked rice and a tossed green salad.

2 T. olive oil
4 boneless, skinless chicken
   cutlets, patted dry
salt and pepper to taste
1/4 c. maple syrup

1 T. orange marmalade
juice of 1 lemon
Garnish: chopped fresh parsley
   or sliced green onions

Heat oil in a non-stick skillet over medium-high heat. When hot, add chicken; season with salt and pepper. Cook until chicken is golden on both sides and juices run clear when pierced. Transfer to a warm platter; keep warm. In a small saucepan over medium heat, heat maple syrup until bubbly; stir in marmalade. Simmer until sauce thickens, about one minute. Ladle sauce over chicken; sprinkle with lemon juice. Garnish as desired. Serves 4.

Begin a new and heartfelt Thanksgiving tradition. Ask your friends & family to bring along an extra food package or can to dinner, then deliver them to a local food pantry.

Sloppy Joe Special

Mary Kay Hahn
Willoughby, OH

This recipe has been a family favorite for over forty years. Back in the early 1970s, I was a home economist for the electric company. We used this recipe to demonstrate the features of an electric range to Home Ec classes and scout troops. It uses the oven, the surface units and the broiler...and it tastes great too!

8-1/2 oz. pkg. cornbread mix
1/3 c. milk
1 egg, beaten
1 lb. ground beef
6-oz. can tomato paste

1-1/2 oz. pkg. Sloppy Joe
  seasoning mix
1-1/4 c. water
8-oz. pkg. shredded Cheddar
  cheese

Prepare cornbread mix with milk and egg according to package directions. Grease the bottom of a 13"x9" baking pan; pour batter into pan. Bake at 350 degrees for 8 minutes, or until golden. Meanwhile, brown beef in a skillet over medium heat; drain. Stir in tomato paste, seasoning mix and water; bring to a boil. Reduce heat and let simmer for 5 minutes. Spoon beef mixture over warm cornbread; sprinkle with cheese. Place under broiler just long enough to melt cheese. Cut into squares to serve. Makes 6 to 12 servings.

For the easiest-ever fall centerpiece, simply lay a wreath of
autumn leaves or bittersweet berries on the table and
set a pumpkin in the center...so clever!

Mains

Pumpkin Joes

Bridget Schultz
Naperville, IL

Serve on your favorite toasty buns with a side of sweet potato fries.

1-1/2 lbs. ground beef sirloin
1 onion, chopped
12-oz. bottle chili sauce
1/2 c. canned pumpkin

10-3/4 oz. can tomato soup
1 T. pumpkin pie spice
1 t. salt
1 t. pepper

Brown beef with onion in a skillet over medium heat. Drain; stir in remaining ingredients. Reduce heat; cover and simmer, stirring occasionally, for one hour. Serves 6 to 8.

I have fond memories of trips to our family cabin in the Finger Lakes region of New York. The trees were always beautiful hues of orange, red and gold. My grandfather would take me for walks in the woods, where he showed me the different kinds of leaves. We would pick apples together from the wild apple trees and colorful leaves to press in wax paper. Sometimes we'd find a deer track and make a plaster cast of it. When we returned to the cabin, Mom and Grandma would have cider and doughnuts ready. Somehow, I also always came back with wild burrs stuck all over me that Mom had to pick out of my clothes and hair. Those were the days!

-Graceann Federico, Ridgeland, SC

Russian Hot Pot

Laura Nassar
Placentia, CA

This recipe was handed down from my grandmother. My family loves it for dinner on a chilly autumn day! Serve with warm, crusty French bread and lots of butter...so satisfying.

2 c. water
2 cubes beef bouillon
1 lb. redskin potatoes, cut into
   1/2-inch cubes
1 lb. cabbage, cut into 1/2-inch
   cubes

1 onion, quartered
16-oz. can whole tomatoes,
   drained
1-1/2 lbs. lean ground beef

Combine water and bouillon in a Dutch oven; bring to a boil over medium-high heat. Add potatoes and increase heat to high. Add cabbage, onion and tomatoes, breaking up tomatoes with your fingers. Add uncooked beef, crumbling it up. Let contents of pan boil for about 30 seconds; stir to mix well. Cover; reduce heat and simmer about 30 minutes, until potatoes are tender. To serve, ladle into soup bowls. Serves 6.

Hearty stews are simple to make and taste even better the next day...why not make a double batch? Let it cool thoroughly, then cover and refrigerate for up to three days, or spoon into a large plastic freezer bag and freeze. A second terrific meal for almost no extra effort!

Skillet Meatloaf

JoAnn

*Making meatloaf on the stovetop saves a lot
of time...a non-stick skillet makes clean-up a snap!*

2 eggs, beaten
1/2 c. catsup
1 T. Worcestershire sauce
1 t. mustard
salt and pepper to taste
2 c. saltine cracker crumbs
1 onion, chopped
Optional: 1/2 c. celery, thinly
   sliced, and 1/2 c. carrot,
   peeled and thinly sliced
2 lbs. lean ground beef
Optional: additional catsup

In a large bowl, whisk together eggs, catsup, Worcestershire sauce,
mustard, salt and pepper. Add cracker crumbs, onion, celery and
carrot, if using; combine well. Add beef and mix well, using your
hands. Pat into a 10" non-stick skillet. Top with catsup as desired.
Cover and cook over medium heat for 8 minutes. Reduce heat to
low. Cover and cook an additional 15 to 20 minutes, until beef is no
longer pink in the center. Drain; let stand a few minutes before slicing.
Serves 8.

Everyone knows mashed potatoes are the perfect side dish for
savory meatloaf. Try a delicious secret the next time you make
the potatoes...substitute equal parts chicken broth and cream
for the milk in any favorite recipe.

Hearty Squash Casserole

Sarina Skidmore
Springfield, MO

A family favorite on chilly evenings...super for potlucks too.

1 c. yellow squash, shredded
2 potatoes, peeled and sliced
1/3 c. red onion, chopped
14-1/2 oz. can diced tomatoes
    with basil, garlic & oregano,
    drained
1/2 c. butter, melted

8-oz. pkg. chicken-flavored
    stuffing mix
1-1/2 lbs. ground beef, browned
    and drained
2 10-3/4 oz. cans cream of
    mushroom soup
1-1/3 c. water

Lightly spray a 3-1/2 quart casserole dish with non-stick vegetable spray. Layer squash, potatoes, onion and tomatoes in dish; set aside. In a separate bowl, toss together melted butter and stuffing. Spoon over tomatoes. In another bowl, mix ground beef, soups and water; spoon over stuffing mixture. Cover and bake at 350 degrees for one hour, or until bubbly and vegetables are tender. Makes 6 to 8 servings.

On Turkey Day, there's really no need for fancy appetizers...just set out a bowl of unshelled walnuts or pecans and a nutcracker! Guests will busy themselves cracking nuts to snack on while you put the finishing touches on dinner.

Mains

Cheesy Ground Beef Bake

Marilynn Dunlap
Tinley Park, IL

This quick, filling recipe has been a family favorite ever since it was given to my mom more than seventy-five years ago.

1 lb. ground beef
1/2 c. onion, chopped
I/2 c. green pepper, chopped
Optional: 3/8 t. garlic salt

16-oz. pkg. elbow macaroni, uncooked
8-oz. jar pasteurized process cheese sauce

Brown together beef, onion and pepper in a skillet over medium heat. Drain; sprinkle with garlic salt, if using. While beef mixture is cooking, prepare macaroni according to package directions; drain. Place macaroni in a 2-quart casserole dish sprayed with non-stick vegetable spray. Add beef mixture; spoon cheese sauce evenly over top. Bake, uncovered, at 350 degrees for 30 minutes, or until hot and bubbly. Serves 4 to 6.

For baked casseroles, cook pasta for the shortest cooking time recommended on the package. It's not necessary to rinse the cooked pasta...just drain it well.

Stuffed French Bread

Tara Diaz
Naples, UT

A favorite recipe my Aunt Paula taught me to make...the very first meal I prepared all by myself! You can substitute any cream soup you like for the cream of broccoli.

1 lb. ground beef
salt and pepper to taste
1 loaf French bread
2 10-3/4 oz. cans cream of
   broccoli soup

2 c. shredded Colby-Jack cheese,
   divided

In a skillet over medium heat, brown beef. Drain; season with salt and pepper and set aside. Cut top off loaf horizontally, 1/3 from the top. Hollow out inside of loaf, being careful not to make the walls too thin; set loaf aside. Place pulled-out bread in a large bowl and tear into chunks. Add beef, soup and one cup cheese; mix well. Spoon mixture into hollowed-out loaf; top with remaining cheese. Bake, uncovered, at 350 degrees for 25 to 30 minutes, until heated through. Replace top of loaf for the last 10 minutes of baking. Slice and serve. Makes 8 servings.

Set a short pillar candle on a food can inside a clear glass punch bowl, then fill the bowl with shiny apples...a lovely centerpiece in a snap for an autumn dinner table.

Savory Beef & Peppers

Cheri Emery
Quincy, IL

This dish is especially delicious on a chilly autumn evening.
It's really a tummy warmer!

1-1/2 lbs. beef round steak,
    cut into thin strips
2 T. oil
1/2 t. garlic powder
1/4 c. onion, chopped
2 green peppers, chopped

10-1/2 oz. can beef broth
1/4 c. cold water
3 T. cornstarch
1/2 t. salt
1/4 t. pepper
cooked rice

In a skillet over medium heat, brown beef on all sides in oil. Sprinkle with garlic powder; cook 2 more minutes. Drain; add onion, peppers and broth to skillet. Cover; reduce heat and simmer for 30 minutes, or until cooked to desired tenderness. In a cup, mix together water and cornstarch; gradually stir into mixture in skillet along with salt and pepper. Cook, stirring often, until gravy is thick and shiny. Serve over cooked rice. Serves 6.

It's a snap to slice uncooked meat when it is slightly frozen...pop it in the freezer for 10 to 15 minutes before slicing.

Tailgaters' Penne Pasta

Debi King
Reisterstown, MD

This started out as a holiday favorite that I began making for
Baltimore Ravens football tailgating. We all love it!

1-1/2 lbs. ground beef
1 lb. hot pork sausage, sliced
   1/2-inch thick
1 c. onion, chopped
2 t. dried oregano
16-oz. pkg. mini penne pasta,
   uncooked

2 10-3/4 oz. cans Cheddar
   cheese soup
2 10-3/4 oz. cans tomato soup
2 c. water
4 slices Cheddar cheese, sliced
   diagonally

In a large, deep oven-safe skillet over medium heat, brown beef,
sausage, onion and oregano. Break up meat with a spatula as it
cooks; drain. Meanwhile, cook pasta according to package directions;
drain. Add pasta, soups and water to mixture in skillet; stir well.
Cover skillet and place in a cold oven. Turn to 400 degrees and bake
for 40 minutes, or until hot. Remove from oven; arrange cheese slices
on top. Return to oven and bake 3 to 4 additional minutes, until
cheese melts. Serves 10.

Spice up your favorite ranch salad dressing. To one cup of ranch
salad dressing, whisk in 1/2 teaspoon ground cumin and
1/4 teaspoon chili powder. Let stand a few minutes for flavors
to blend. Super for salads...divine for dipping!

Mains

Smoked Sausage & Barley Stew

Dani Simmers
Kendallville, IN

You've got to try this one! It's a hearty, taste-tempting blend of winter veggies and smoked sausage, thickened with yummy barley. My very good friend Beth introduced this to me on a chilly day...it is a wonderful warmer-upper.

1 lb. smoked pork sausage, cut
    into bite-size pieces
1 onion, chopped
2-1/2 c. beef broth
2 to 3 carrots, peeled and sliced
1/4 head cabbage, cut into
    one-inch cubes

1/4 c. quick-cooking barley,
    uncooked
14-1/2 oz. can whole tomatoes,
    drained and chopped

In a Dutch oven over medium heat, sauté sausage and onion until onion is tender, about 6 minutes. Drain; stir in remaining ingredients except tomatoes. Bring to a boil. Reduce heat, cover and simmer for 25 minutes, or until vegetables are tender. Stir in tomatoes just before serving; warm through. Serves 4 to 6.

If it's Thanksgiving now, Christmas can't be far away. Why not double any festive must-have casseroles or side dishes and freeze half for Christmas dinner...you'll be so glad you did!

Apple Orchard Pork Chops

Diana Bulls
Reedley, CA

I clipped this recipe out of the newspaper years ago. We all love it,
especially in the fall when fresh-picked apples are abundant.

4 apples, peeled, cored and
   cubed
1/4 c. lemon juice
1/4 t. nutmeg
1 to 2 T. oil

4 pork chops
salt and pepper to taste
1/4 c. apple cider or juice
Optional: 1 T. butter

Place apples in a bowl. Sprinkle with lemon juice and nutmeg; set
aside. Add oil to a large skillet over medium-high heat. Add pork
chops; sprinkle with salt and pepper. Cook for about 6 minutes. Turn
chops over; brown on other side for about 5 minutes, or until chops
are no longer pink in the center. Add apples; cover and cook until
apples are tender. Remove chops to a serving platter; keep warm. To
make sauce, add cider or juice to skillet. Increase heat while stirring
and scraping up any browned bits. For a richer sauce, swirl in butter
just before serving. Spoon sauce over pork chops. Makes 4 servings.

For a side dish that practically cooks itself, fill aluminum foil
packets with sliced fresh veggies. Top with seasoning salt
and two ice cubes, seal and bake at 450 degrees for
20 to 25 minutes. Delicious!

Mains

Autumn Pork Chop Dinner

Jackie Flood
Geneseo, NY

My older sister gave me this recipe and it's become a family favorite.
Don't let the name fool you...it's tasty any time of year!

6 boneless pork chops
1 T. oil
6-oz. pkg. chicken-flavored
   stuffing mix

21-oz. can apple pie filling

In a skillet over medium heat, lightly brown pork chops in oil; drain. Prepare stuffing according to package directions; set aside. Spread pie filling in the bottom of a 13"x9" baking pan sprayed with non-stick vegetable spray. Top pie filling with chops, then stuffing. Cover with aluminum foil. Bake at 375 degrees for 30 minutes; uncover and bake an additional 10 minutes, or until chops are cooked through. Serves 6.

Pick up some paper plates and cups in seasonal designs...they'll make dinner fun when you're in a hurry and clean-up will be a breeze.

Can-Do Ham Dinner

Jewel Sharpe
Raleigh, NC

This is a quick and very tasty dinner. We make it a lot when we go camping. Delicious, especially when sitting around the campfire.

1 T. oil
2 to 3-lb. canned ham, sliced
1 to 2 16-oz. cans yams,
   drained

pepper to taste
8-oz. can crushed pineapple,
   drained
1/2 t. pumpkin pie spice

Heat oil in a skillet over medium heat. Add ham slices; heat through. Turn ham over; pour yams over ham. Sprinkle with pepper. Top with pineapple; sprinkle with pumpkin pie spice. Reduce heat and simmer until pineapple is caramelized, about 15 minutes. Serves 4 to 6.

Remember to tote along some blankets or folding stools when you go camping...there's nothing like sitting around a glowing campfire stargazing, swapping stories and just savoring time together with friends & family!

Mains

Nanelle's Potatoes & Ham

Karen Miller
Baytown, TX

*My friend at work shared this recipe with me one day. It became
a hit with my family...yours is sure to like it too!*

1/2 c. butter
5 potatoes, peeled and chopped
1 onion, chopped
1/2 lb. cooked ham, chopped

2 14-1/2 oz. cans green beans,
   drained
14-oz. can chicken broth
salt and pepper to taste

Melt butter in a skillet over medium heat. Sauté potatoes and onion
until slightly tender, about 10 minutes. Add ham, beans and broth to
skillet. Cover and simmer until potatoes are tender, about 15 minutes.
Add salt and pepper to taste. Serves 6.

As autumn evenings turn dark, light a candle or two at the
family dinner table. It'll make an ordinary meal seem special!

Harvest Pork Skillet

Regina Vining
Warwick, RI

A speedy skillet dish my daughters like so much,
they don't mind all the veggies! On the table in less than
thirty minutes...you can't beat it!

4 boneless pork chops, diced
2 to 3 t. oil
12-oz. jar pork gravy
2 T. catsup

8 redskin potatoes, diced
2 c. frozen mixed vegetables
salt and pepper to taste

In a large skillet over medium heat, brown pork chops in oil. Drain;
stir in gravy, catsup and potatoes. Cover and simmer for 10 minutes.
Stir in vegetables; cook for 10 to 15 minutes longer, until vegetables
are tender and pork is cooked through. Serves 4.

Don't forget the nametags at your extended family's
Thanksgiving dinner! Use a different color of tag for
each family...it'll be a snap to know which branch of
the family tree each person comes from.

Mains

Rosemary Pork Loin

Carrie O'Shea
Marina Del Rey, CA

I grow rosemary in my garden, so I'm always looking for recipes to use it in. I've tried many chicken dishes, but I had never paired pork and rosemary until my sister shared this recipe with me. Yum!

1 T. butter
1-lb. pork tenderloin, cut into
   8 1-inch-thick slices
1 c. sliced mushrooms
2 T. onion, finely chopped
1-1/2 T. fresh rosemary,
   chopped

1 clove garlic, minced
salt and pepper to taste
1 T. cooking sherry or apple
   juice
Garnish: fresh rosemary sprigs

Melt butter in a heavy skillet over medium-high heat. Brown pork slices quickly, about one minute on each side. Remove pork to a serving plate, reserving drippings in skillet. Add remaining ingredients except sherry or juice and garnish to skillet. Cook and stir over low heat for several minutes, until mushrooms and onion are almost tender. Stir in sherry or juice. Return pork to skillet; spoon mushroom mixture over pork. Cover; simmer 3 to 4 more minutes. Garnish with sprigs of rosemary. Serves 4.

Turn a small pumpkin or winter squash into an unexpected floral centerpiece. Carefully cut a hole in the top and scoop out the insides. Set it on a dish, slip a water-filled tumbler inside and tuck in a bouquet of seasonal flowers...so pretty!

BBQ Roasted Salmon

Tara Horton
Gooseberry Patch

*By far, this is my favorite salmon recipe. It has great flavor
and I always have the spices on hand.*

2 T. brown sugar, packed
4 t. chili powder
3/4 t. ground cumin

1/2 t. salt
1/4 t. cinnamon
4 salmon fillets

Combine sugar and spices in a shallow dish. Dredge fillets in sugar
mixture. Spray an 11"x7" baking pan with non-stick vegetable spray.
Arrange fillets in pan. Bake, uncovered, at 400 degrees for 12 minutes,
or until fish flakes easily with a fork. Serves 4.

Baked Crumbed Haddock

Michelle Waddington
New Bedford, MA

*Delicious! Serve with buttery mashed potatoes and
steamed broccoli for a down-home dinner.*

2 5-1/2 oz. pkgs. onion &
   garlic croutons

1 c. butter, melted
3 lbs. haddock fillets

Finely grind croutons in a food processor. Toss together croutons
and butter. Place fish in a greased 13"x9" baking pan. Sprinkle
crouton mixture over fish. Bake, uncovered, at 350 degrees for about
30 minutes, or until fish flakes easily with a fork. Serves 6 to 8.

Host a neighborhood spruce-up! Everyone can help trim bushes
and pull bloomed-out annuals...kids can even rake leaves.
End with a simple supper for all.

Mains

Snapper in a Snap

Cheri Maxwell
Gulf Breeze, FL

*Here on the Gulf Coast we eat a lot of fresh red snapper,
so I was happy to find a new way to serve it. This recipe takes
just a little of this & that to create a delicious dish.*

1/2 c. lemon juice
1/4 c. rice wine vinegar
2 T. olive oil
2 T. honey

2 t. Dijon mustard
2 t. ground ginger
1/2 c. green onions, chopped
1 lb. red snapper fillets

In a shallow bowl, whisk together all ingredients except onions and
fish fillets; stir in onions. Heat a non-stick skillet over medium heat.
Dip fish fillets in lemon juice mixture to coat both sides; add to skillet.
Cook for 2 to 3 minutes on each side. Pour remaining mixture into
skillet. Reduce heat and simmer for 2 to 3 minutes, until fish flakes
easily with a fork. Serves 4.

Stir up a simple side of rice pilaf. In a saucepan, bring 2 cups
chicken broth to a boil. Stir in one cup long-cooking rice;
reduce heat, cover and simmer for 20 to 25 minutes. Meanwhile,
sauté 1/2 cup each sliced mushrooms and green onions in a little
oil just until tender. When rice is done, stir in mushroom
mixture, a dash of soy sauce and 1/2 cup snipped fresh
parsley; fluff with a fork. Serves 4.

Creamy Fettuccine Alfredo

Joseph Balcer
Glenshaw, PA

This recipe is easy and inexpensive...it's delicious too! Make it heartier by adding grilled chicken, sautéed shrimp or steamed broccoli.

16-oz. pkg. fettuccine pasta,
   uncooked
1/2 c. butter, softened
1/2 c. grated Parmesan cheese

1/2 c. light cream
salt and pepper to taste
Garnish: additional grated
   Parmesan cheese

Prepare fettuccine according to package directions, using the shortest cooking time given; drain. Return fettuccine to cooking pot and add butter; toss until well-coated. Add Parmesan cheese; toss to coat. Add cream, tossing to combine well. Add salt and pepper to taste. Serve with additional Parmesan cheese. Serves 6.

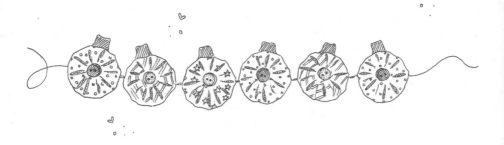

Set aside time for a little crafting after all the tasty food has been enjoyed. Choose an easy theme, like making notecards or simple ornaments, and everyone can bring along their favorite supplies to share.

Mains

Ravioli & Meatballs Pronto

Hope Davenport
Portland, TX

Our younger two kids get so excited when this is on the menu...you'd think I was serving chocolate cake! It is a nice change from spaghetti and just as quick & easy. Try it with other kinds of cheese too, like sharp Cheddar or Colby Jack...yum!

25-oz. pkg. frozen cheese-filled
  ravioli
20-oz. pkg. frozen cooked
  meatballs, thawed

28-oz. jar spaghetti sauce
Optional: garlic salt to taste
1-1/2 c. shredded mozzarella
  cheese

Prepare ravioli according to package directions. Drain and place in a greased 13"x9" baking pan. Top with meatballs and sauce. Sprinkle with garlic salt, if desired, and cheese. Bake, uncovered, at 375 degrees for 35 minutes, or until heated through. Serves 6.

Autumn is my favorite season. I remember as a child
having to help rake leaves...yuck! But there was always a plus
to the chore...afterwards, we got to wrap potatoes in aluminum
foil and bake them in the burning leaves. Potatoes tasted extra
delicious when they were baked in the piles of fallen leaves
that lined our street. We no longer can burn leaves in the city,
but the memory will always be there.

-Monica Stepke, South Boardman, MI

Italian Crescent Casserole

Amanda Gladden
Oneonta, AL

*My family truly enjoys this crust-topped casserole...we like it
better than spaghetti!*

1-1/2 to 2 lbs. ground beef
  or turkey
1 onion, chopped
16-oz. jar spaghetti sauce
8-oz. pkg. shredded mozzarella
  cheese

8-oz. container sour cream
8-oz. tube refrigerated crescent
  rolls
2 T. butter, melted
1/2 c. grated Parmesan cheese

Brown meat and onion in a large skillet over medium heat. Drain;
rinse meat mixture under hot water and return to skillet. Stir in
sauce; simmer for about 10 minutes. Transfer mixture to a greased
13"x9" baking pan. Combine mozzarella cheese and sour cream;
spoon over mixture in pan. Unroll crescent rolls but do not separate;
place on top of mixture in pan. Drizzle rolls with melted butter;
sprinkle with Parmesan cheese. Bake, uncovered, at 350 degrees for
about 30 minutes, until bubbly and golden. Serves 8.

Keep a warm quilt or blanket-stitched throw in the car
for autumn picnics and football games...perfect for
staying warm & cozy.

Favorite Turkey Spaghetti

Susi Dickinson
Prentice, WI

I make this hearty dish with leftover Thanksgiving turkey...it's a winner at our house!

8-oz. pkg. spaghetti pasta,
  uncooked and broken up
2 c. cooked turkey or chicken,
  chopped
10-3/4 oz. can cream of chicken
  soup
1 c. milk

1/4 t. salt
1/4 t. pepper
2 c. shredded Cheddar cheese
1-1/2 c. round buttery crackers,
  crushed
2 T. butter, diced

Cook spaghetti according to package directions; drain. Meanwhile, in a bowl, combine turkey or chicken, soup, milk, salt, pepper and cheese. Add spaghetti to turkey mixture; mix well and place in a greased 13"x9" baking pan. Sprinkle with cracker crumbs; dot with butter. Bake, uncovered, at 350 degrees for about 45 minutes, until heated through. Serves 6 to 8.

If hungry kids are getting underfoot while you're preparing Thanksgiving dinner, let them make some turkey track snacks! Spread softened cheese spread on a round buttery cracker and arrange three chow mein noodles on top for the "track." Place on a platter for tasty nibbling.

Stovetop Lasagna

Tiffany Jones
Locust Grove, AR

Lasagna is a favorite meal at my house. This quick & easy variation on traditional lasagna has all the flavor without much of the effort!

8-oz. pkg. rotini pasta,
  uncooked
1 lb. ground beef
26-oz. jar spaghetti sauce
24-oz. container cream-style
  cottage cheese

8-oz. pkg. shredded mozzarella
  cheese
1 t. Italian seasoning
salt and pepper to taste

Cook rotini according to package directions; drain. Meanwhile, in a large skillet over medium heat, brown beef; drain. Stir in remaining ingredients; cook over low heat until bubbly and cheese is melted. Stir in cooked rotini. Reduce heat to low; simmer for 20 minutes. Serves 4.

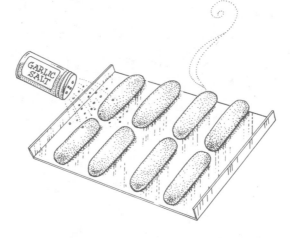

To serve alongside a quick Italian dinner, turn leftover hot dog buns into garlic bread sticks in a jiffy. Spread buns with softened butter, sprinkle with garlic salt and broil until toasty...yum!

Desserts

Grandma's Apple-Nut Dessert

Cindy Pugliese
Wheat Ridge, CO

When my sister Linda and I were growing up, this dessert was served alongside the pumpkin pie on Thanksgiving. We associate this recipe with our grandma, but the recipe originally came from our dad's grandma. Now Linda hosts Thanksgiving, and she always asks me to bring this dessert. It's easy to make and very good!

1-1/2 c. sugar
1 c. all-purpose flour
2 t. baking powder
1/2 t. salt
2 eggs, beaten

1 t. vanilla extract
2 c. tart apples, cored and
   chopped
1 c. walnuts, coarsely chopped
Garnish: whipped cream

Blend together sugar, flour, baking powder and salt in a large bowl. Add remaining ingredients except whipped cream; stir well. Spread in a greased 12"x9" baking pan. Bake, uncovered, at 350 degrees for 30 minutes. Serve topped with dollops of whipped cream. Makes 12 servings.

Halloween has always been special to me. I grew up in a small neighborhood in Tennessee where everyone was very close and looked out for each other. Every year at Halloween, we kids would go trick-or-treating through the neighborhood and then meet together at Mrs. Debra's house. She would have a Halloween party in her garage complete with games like bobbing for apples, feeling the eyeballs (yuck!), fortune telling and more. It was all so much fun!

-Jessica Haggard Crowell, Rainsville, AL

148

Apple Betty

Maria Rogers
Auburn, NY

*A favorite fall dessert in our home. If you're lucky enough
to have some homemade applesauce, use it for real
old-fashioned goodness.*

2-1/4 c. long-cooking oats,
　uncooked
2-1/4 c. all-purpose flour
1-1/2 c. brown sugar, packed

3/4 t. baking soda
1 c. plus 2 T. butter, softened
2-1/2 to 3 c. applesauce

Mix together all ingredients except applesauce. Press 2/3 of mixture
into a lightly greased 13"x9" baking pan. Spread applesauce over oat
mixture in pan. Sprinkle remaining oat mixture over applesauce.
Bake, uncovered, at 350 degrees for 30 to 35 minutes, until golden.
Makes 10 to 12 servings.

Most fruit pies and cobblers can be frozen up to four months
in advance...what a time-saver! Cool completely after baking,
then wrap well in plastic wrap and two layers of aluminum foil
before freezing. To serve, thaw overnight in the fridge, bring to
room temperature and rewarm in the oven.

Sweet Apple Tarts

Jill Ball
Highland, UT

A delicious can't-fail recipe that's perfect for any occasion! Cut the pastry squares with a fluted pastry wheel for a pretty finish.

1 sheet frozen puff pastry,
   thawed
1/2 c. apricot jam
3 to 4 Granny Smith apples,
   peeled, cored and very thinly
   sliced

1/3 c. brown sugar, packed
1/2 t. cinnamon
1/2 c. pistachios, chopped
Garnish: vanilla ice cream

Roll pastry into a 12-inch square on a floured surface. Cut into nine, 3-inch squares. Arrange squares on an ungreased baking sheet; pierce with a fork. Coat each square with a spoonful of jam; arrange apple slices over jam. In a small bowl, combine brown sugar and cinnamon; mix well. Sprinkle over apple slices. Bake at 350 degrees for 10 to 12 minutes, until pastry is golden and apples are crisp-tender. Sprinkle with pistachios. Serve warm, topped with scoops of ice cream. Serves 6.

Be sure to pick up a pint or two of ice cream in pumpkin, cinnamon and other delicious seasonal flavors when they're available...they add that special touch to holiday meals!

Desserts

Apple-Cinnamon Cake

Laura Witham
Anchorage, AK

*Sometimes I get bored in the kitchen and I have to
start experimenting quick! This is the delectable result
of one experiment.*

7-oz. pkg. apple-cinnamon
   muffin mix
1/4 c. milk

1 egg, beaten
1-1/2 T. apple butter
1 T. brown sugar, packed

Combine together all ingredients; mix well. Pour into a greased
8"x8" baking pan. Bake at 350 degrees for 25 to 30 minutes, until
a toothpick tests clean. Cool cake in pan; invert onto a serving plate.
Top with Apple Butter Frosting. Makes 6 servings.

Apple Butter Frosting:

1/2 c. cream cheese, softened
1-1/2 t. apple butter

1-1/2 t. brown sugar, packed

Blend all ingredients together until smooth.

Core apples and pears in a jiffy...cut the fruit in half,
then use a melon baller to scoop out the center.

Harvest Pear Crisp

Elizabeth Shultz
Ankeny, IA

*I combined several recipes to come up with the perfect formula.
My daughter loves helping me with this, because pears are
softer and easier to peel and chop than apples.*

3 c. Bartlett pears, peeled, cored and sliced	1/2 c. plus 2 T. all-purpose flour, divided
3 T. water	1 t. cinnamon, divided
1 T. lemon juice	5 T. chilled butter
1/2 c. sugar, divided	1/4 c. brown sugar, packed

In a bowl, combine pears, water, lemon juice, 1/4 cup sugar,
2 tablespoons flour and 1/2 teaspoon cinnamon. Toss to mix. Spread
in an 8"x8" baking pan sprayed with non-stick vegetable spray. In a
separate bowl, cut together butter, brown sugar and remaining sugar,
flour and cinnamon until crumbly. Sprinkle over pear mixture. Bake
at 350 degrees for 45 minutes, or until pears are tender. Serves 6.

Make some charming tealight jars...a terrific craft for kids.
Brush slightly thinned craft glue over empty baby food jars and
cover with small squares of tissue paper. Brush a little more
thinned glue over the finished jars. When dry, pop a tealight
inside. Glowing harvest shades of orange,
gold and yellow are especially delightful.

Desserts

Maple-Brown Sugar Apple Crumble *Shelly Smith*
Dana, IN

*The smell of this apple dessert in the oven really puts us
in the mood for leaf raking, pumpkin carving and
all our other favorite fall activities.*

5 apples, peeled, cored and
    sliced
2/3 c. maple syrup
1/2 c. butter, softened
1/2 c. brown sugar, packed

3/4 c. all-purpose flour
3/4 c. long-cooking oats,
    uncooked
1/8 t. salt

Place sliced apples in a lightly greased 8"x8" baking pan; drizzle
maple syrup over apples. In a bowl, blend together butter and brown
sugar. Stir in flour, oats and salt until crumbly. Sprinkle butter mixture
over apples. Bake, uncovered, at 375 degrees for 35 minutes, or until
golden and apples are tender. Serves 4.

For an affordable casual get-together, invite friends over
for "just desserts!" Offer two or three simple homebaked
desserts like cobblers, dump cake and fruit pie, ice cream for
topping and a steamy pot of coffee...they'll love it!

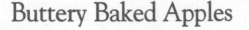

Buttery Baked Apples

Tonya Adams
Magnolia, KY

Mmm! This old-fashioned dessert is also a great side dish with pork chops...it's even good for breakfast.

8 baking apples, cored
1 c. sugar
6 T. butter, sliced
1 T. cold water

1/2 t. vanilla extract
1 T. cornstarch
1/2 c. milk

Place apples in a lightly greased 1-1/2 quart casserole dish. Sprinkle with sugar; dot with butter. Bake, uncovered, at 450 degrees for 20 minutes, or until crisp-tender, basting occasionally with liquid in dish. Remove apples from dish to a separate plate; set aside. Combine water, vanilla and cornstarch in a bowl; stir in milk. Add to liquid in dish, mixing well. Return apples to dish. Bake an additional 8 to 10 minutes, until sauce is thickened. Serves 8.

When I was a young girl, we used to visit my Aunt Sadie and Uncle Ed often. I can still remember their farmhouse in the country with all the beautiful flowers. Aunt Sadie always had something scrumptious baking...you'd smell the aromas filling the kitchen as soon as you walked in! Peach pie, hot cross buns and salt-rising bread were her specialties. And cookies...you just had to eat at least ten of them! Always wearing her full apron, wiping her hands as she welcomed us to her old kitchen table, her face beamed with love as my brothers and I sat on the old wooden chairs. I still think of Aunt Sadie and smell the delicious baked goods fresh from her oven.

-Sandra Richter, South Dayton, NY

Desserts

Taffy Apple Pizza

Brenda Smith
Gooseberry Patch

*An after-school treat I used to make for my kids when
they were younger. A great way to catch up on their day
while enjoying this tasty dessert together!*

18-oz. pkg. refrigerated sugar
   cookie dough
8-oz. pkg. cream cheese,
   softened
1/2 c. brown sugar, packed
1/4 c. creamy or crunchy peanut
   butter

1 t. vanilla extract
2 Granny Smith apples, peeled,
   cored and sliced
1/4 c. caramel ice cream topping
1/2 c. chopped peanuts

Form cookie dough into a ball and place in the center of a greased
14" round pizza pan. Using a lightly floured rolling pin, roll out to a
14-inch circle, about 1/4-inch thick. Bake at 350 degrees for 16 to
18 minutes, until lightly golden. Remove from oven; cool 10 minutes.
Loosen cookie from pan slightly with a serrated knife. Combine cream
cheese, brown sugar, peanut butter and vanilla; mix well and spread
evenly over cookie. Cut apple slices in half and arrange evenly over
cream cheese mixture. Microwave topping on high setting for 30 to
45 seconds, until warm; drizzle evenly over apples. Sprinkle peanuts
over top; cut into wedges. Makes 8 to 10 servings.

Do you have lots of kids coming for an after-game party or
trick-or-treat night? Make it easy with do-it-yourself tacos or
mini pizzas...guests can add their own favorite toppings.
Round out the menu with pitchers of soft drinks and
a yummy dessert pizza. Simple and fun!

Cherry Cobbler

Carol Van Rooy
Ontario, Canada

I've made this scrumptious dessert numerous times and received so many compliments and requests for the recipe! An international friend first shared this with me and since then, I've tweaked it to our family's own taste. We really enjoy it.

21-oz. can cherry pie filling
1 T. lemon juice
1 t. cinnamon
1/2 c. butter, melted

1-1/4 c. all-purpose flour
1/2 c. sugar
2 t. baking powder
1 c. milk

Mix together pie filling, lemon juice and cinnamon; set aside. In a separate bowl, mix together remaining ingredients with a fork. Spread batter into a lightly greased 13"x9" glass baking pan. Carefully spoon pie filling mixture evenly over batter. Bake at 325 degrees for 25 minutes. Increase oven to 350 degrees; bake for an additional 10 minutes, or until golden and batter has risen over the top of the pie filling. Serves 8 to 10.

After a hearty meal, offer mini portions of rich cake, cobbler or pie layered in small glasses with whipped topping and a crunchy topping. Guests can take "just a taste" of something sweet or sample several yummy treats.

Desserts

Quick Peach Crumble

Susie Clayton
South Saint Paul, MN

My go-to recipe whenever I need a dessert in a hurry. Serve it warm with a scoop of vanilla ice cream...luscious!

15-oz. can diced peaches
18-1/2 oz. pkg. yellow cake mix

2 t. cinnamon
1/4 c. butter, melted

Pour peaches and their juice into a greased 13"x9" baking pan. Sprinkle dry cake mix and cinnamon on top. Drizzle melted butter over all. Bake at 375 degrees for 35 to 40 minutes, until golden on top and bubbly on the sides. Serves 12.

Yummy Pineapple Pies

Shannon Ward
Winona, WV

I loved these sweet pies when I was growing up...I still do! I remember Mom making them every Thanksgiving and Christmas. As a kid, I'd look at these fluffy pies and think, oh my, these look like the kind of cream pie a comedian gets in the face!

2 9-inch pie crusts
14-oz. can sweetened
   condensed milk
16-oz. container frozen
   whipped topping, thawed

2 20-oz. cans crushed
   pineapple, drained
2 to 4 T. lemon juice

Bake pie crusts according to package directions; set aside to cool. In a bowl, combine remaining ingredients; mix well. Spoon mixture into the pie crusts. Cover and refrigerate for several hours to overnight before slicing. Makes 2 pies; each serves 6 to 8.

Favorite Cranberry Crunch

Sharon Winters
Anderson, SC

This dessert is from a close friend and neighbor in the Chicago area. We shared Thanksgiving and Christmas every year, so when we moved south I brought along the recipe to continue the tradition.

3 c. McIntosh apples, cored and
   coarsely chopped
2 c. cranberries
3/4 c. sugar
1-1/2 c. long-cooking oats,
   uncooked

3/4 c. chopped pecans
1/2 c. light brown sugar, packed
1/3 c. all-purpose flour
1/2 c. butter, melted

Toss apples, cranberries and sugar together; put into a lightly greased 13"x9" baking pan. Mix together remaining ingredients except butter; pour over apple mixture. Drizzle with butter. Bake at 350 degrees for 45 minutes. Makes 8 to 10 servings.

For a sweet & salty party snack that's ready in minutes,
serve a tub of caramel apple dip with apple slices and
mini pretzel twists. Yummy!

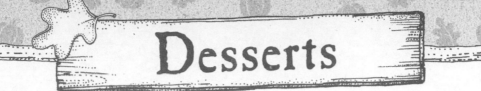

Apple Orchard Cake

Linda Vogt
North Las Vegas, NV

*I start baking this simple dessert for family & friends
as soon as autumn arrives. It gives me a good excuse to head
over to the local orchard to pick my favorite crisp apples.*

1 c. sugar
1/2 c. butter, melted and cooled
   slightly
3 eggs, beaten
2 c. graham cracker crumbs

2 to 3 apples, peeled, cored and
   diced
Optional: 3/4 c. chopped
   walnuts
Garnish: powdered sugar

Stir together sugar, butter and eggs in a bowl. Stir in graham cracker
crumbs, apples and walnuts, if using, until blended well. Spread
batter in a greased 8"x8" baking pan. Bake at 350 degrees for 40 to
45 minutes, until firm to the touch. Sprinkle generously with
powdered sugar. Cool; cut into squares. Makes 4 to 6 servings.

Dress up a plain cake...lay a paper doily or a holiday stencil
on top, then sprinkle with powdered sugar. So dainty,
yet so simple a child can do it!

Creamy Cookie Dessert

Dawn Henderson
Prospect, OH

A yummy ice cream-like dessert from such ordinary ingredients...friends will never believe how simple this is to make!

18-oz. pkg. chocolate sandwich cookies, divided
8-oz. pkg. cream cheese, softened
3.4-oz. pkg. instant vanilla pudding mix
2 c. milk
1 c. powdered sugar
8-oz. container frozen whipped topping, thawed

Set aside 6 to 7 cookies for garnish; crush remaining cookies. Spread 1/4 of crushed cookies in the bottom of a lightly greased 13"x9" glass baking pan; set aside. In a large bowl, whip cream cheese with an electric mixer on medium speed. In a separate bowl, whisk together dry pudding mix and milk for 2 minutes, until thickened; add to cream cheese along with powdered sugar and whipped topping. Beat until well blended. Spoon a layer of cream cheese mixture over cookies; add another layer of crushed cookies and another layer of cream cheese mixture. Repeat once more, for a total of 3 layers. Arrange reserved whole cookies on top. Cover and chill for 2 hours before serving. Keep refrigerated. Serves 10 to 12.

Dress up desserts or baked sweet potatoes with spoonfuls of pecan praline topping...delectable! Combine one cup chopped pecans, 2 tablespoons brown sugar and one tablespoon corn syrup. Stir well and spread on a buttered baking sheet. Bake at 350 degrees, stirring occasionally, for 7 to 10 minutes, until golden. Cool for 15 minutes, then crumble. Topping may be refrigerated, covered, for up to a month.

Desserts

Holy Cow Cake

Karen Stinson
Hendersonville, TN

Holy cow, this is a good cake! It's easy to make yet rich-tasting and impressive...I bet you'll love it as much as I do.

18-1/2 oz. pkg. German
  chocolate cake mix
14-oz. can sweetened
  condensed milk
12-1/4 oz. jar caramel ice cream
  topping
2.1-oz. chocolate-covered crispy
  peanut butter candy bar,
  crushed and divided

8-oz. container frozen whipped
  topping, thawed
8-oz. pkg. cream cheese,
  softened
1 c. sugar

Prepare cake mix according to package directions; bake in a greased 13"x9" baking pan. While cake is baking, stir together condensed milk and caramel topping; set aside. Remove cake from oven. While cake is still hot, poke holes in top with a wooden spoon handle or skewer. Pour condensed milk mixture over cake; sprinkle with half of crushed candy bar. Refrigerate 2 to 3 hours. Mix together remaining ingredients until smooth; spread over chilled cake. Sprinkle with remaining candy bar. Keep refrigerated. Makes 16 to 20 servings.

Cake balls...kids of all ages love 'em! Make some in a jiffy with this quick tip. Insert treat sticks in unglazed cake-type doughnut holes and dip in melted white or semi-sweet chocolate coating. Add candy sprinkles just for fun and stand them in a tall vase for easy serving...done!

German Chocolate Pound Cake

Wanda Freeman
Krum, TX

*This is my tried & true dessert for every potluck and
social...it's so easy to make, bakes up beautifully and tastes
scrumptious. Everyone loves it!*

18-1/2 oz. pkg. German
   chocolate cake mix
3 eggs, beaten
1 c. water

1/3 c. oil
16-oz. can coconut-pecan
   frosting
Garnish: powdered sugar

Spray a Bundt® pan with non-stick vegetable spray; place on a baking
sheet and set aside. In a bowl, combine dry cake mix, eggs, water and
oil. Stir until well blended; beat with an electric mixer on medium
speed for 2 minutes. Slowly beat in frosting until blended. Pour into
prepared pan. Bake at 350 degrees for about 55 minutes, testing for
doneness with a toothpick. Allow cake to cool in pan for 5 minutes;
invert onto a serving plate and allow to cool completely. Dust with
powdered sugar before serving.

Whip up a stack of seasonal coasters in just minutes! Cut
autumn leaf shapes from thick wool felt, using a leaf-shaped
cookie cutter or a real leaf as a pattern. So pretty on the
Thanksgiving table in rich shades of gold and brown.

Desserts

Easy Pumpkin Pound Cake

Carolyn Russell
Clyde, NC

My family loves pumpkin! So, I was happy to find this speedy three-ingredient recipe for a pumpkin pound cake. People ask me for this recipe all the time. Around the holidays, I bake one every week to take to all our favorite events. At a fundraiser, one of my cakes went for twenty-five dollars...we were all so excited!

18-1/2 oz. pkg. yellow cake mix
30-oz. can pumpkin pie mix

16-oz. can cream cheese
   frosting

Beat together dry cake mix and pumpkin in a large bowl. Spread batter in a 12"x10" baking pan sprayed with non-stick vegetable spray. Bake at 350 degrees for 25 to 30 minutes, until a toothpick tests clean. Cool; spread with frosting. Serves 12 to 20.

For a little extra sweetness, drizzle a powdered sugar glaze over freshly-baked cakes, pies and cookies. It's easy...just add 2 tablespoons milk to 1-1/2 cups powdered sugar and stir until smooth.

Lillie's Date Pudding

Sharon Beatu
Cookeville, TN

This is an old family favorite handed down by my
Great-Grandma Lillie. Our Thanksgiving and Christmas holidays
wouldn't be the same without it!

2 c. all-purpose flour
2 c. sugar
2 c. chopped dates
1 c. chopped pecans
1 T. baking powder

1 c. milk
2 c. brown sugar, packed
2 T. butter, softened
1-1/2 c. boiling water

In a large bowl, mix together flour, sugar, dates, pecans, baking powder and milk; set aside. Combine brown sugar, butter and boiling water in a separate large bowl. Pour flour mixture over brown sugar mixture. Stir well and transfer to a greased deep 9"x9" baking pan. Bake at 350 degrees for 40 minutes. Makes 12 servings.

When my husband and I were first married, we decided we would decorate for fall, as it has always been one of our favorite times of the year. We began by collecting pumpkins. Twenty years later, we have dozens of pumpkins in different colors, sizes and materials...metal pumpkins, ceramic pumpkins, fabric pumpkins and twig pumpkins. We even have "wall art" pumpkins! From October 1st until we decorate for Christmas, we have pumpkins in every room of the house. We love it! And we love watching the smiles on everyone who comes into our home as they start noticing them all.

-Denise Collier, Mena, AR

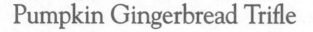

Pumpkin Gingerbread Trifle

Cathy Forbes
Hutchinson, KS

Something different from that same old pumpkin pie! This luscious dessert goes quickly at every covered-dish supper...try it and see!

14-1/2 oz. pkg. gingerbread
  cake mix
3.4-oz. pkg. instant vanilla
  pudding mix
2 c. milk
15-oz. can pumpkin

1/2 t. cinnamon
16-oz. container frozen whipped
  topping, thawed and divided
3 1.4-oz. chocolate-covered
  toffee candy bars, crushed

Prepare and bake cake mix according to package directions. Cool; tear or cut cake into large chunks and set aside. Whisk together dry pudding mix and milk for 2 minutes, until thickened; gently stir in pumpkin and cinnamon. In a clear glass trifle bowl, layer half each of cake chunks, pudding mixture and whipped topping. Repeat layers, ending with topping. Garnish with crushed candy bars. Cover and refrigerate at least 3 hours before serving. Makes 12 to 16 servings.

Decorate cakes and trifles with a sparkling bunch of sugared grapes...it's easier than it looks and so pretty on a dessert buffet. Brush grapes with light corn syrup, then sprinkle generously with sanding sugar and allow to dry.

Sweet Potato Pudding

Jennie Pegram
Glen Allen, VA

I first got this yummy recipe more than thirty years ago from a friend at church. This is the dish I take to most holiday celebrations. It can be put together ahead of time and baked at the last minute.

2 eggs, beaten
1 c. sugar
1-1/2 c. evaporated milk
2 t. vanilla extract
1/8 t. salt
2 c. sweet potatoes, peeled and grated
1/4 c. sweetened flaked coconut

Beat together eggs and sugar until light. Add remaining ingredients, mixing well. Pour into a buttered 1-1/2 quart casserole dish. Bake at 350 degrees for 25 to 45 minutes, until firm. Makes 6 to 8 servings.

Impossible Coconut Pie

Susan Hanenberg
West Milford, NJ

This pie makes its own crust! One of my most requested desserts...and it's so easy.

2 c. milk
4 eggs
1 c. sugar
1 t. vanilla extract
1/2 c. biscuit baking mix
1/4 c. butter, softened
1 c. shredded coconut

Pour all ingredients into a blender; blend for 2 to 3 minutes. Pour into a buttered 9" to 10" pie plate. Bake at 350 degrees for 45 minutes, until set. Makes 6 to 8 servings.

Set a filled pie plate on a baking sheet before popping it in the oven. The baking sheet catches any drips and helps the pie's bottom crust bake more evenly.

Easy Pumpkin Pudding

Dee Ann Ice
Delaware, OH

This recipe was given to me by a co-worker and friend. Even the kids can prepare it, but don't be fooled by its simplicity. It is truly delicious!

5.9-oz. pkg. instant vanilla
    pudding mix
1-1/2 c. milk
1 c. canned pumpkin pie mix
1/2 t. pumpkin pie spice

16-oz. container frozen whipped
    topping, thawed and divided
1 c. gingersnap or graham
    cracker crumbs, divided

In a large bowl, with an electric mixer on low speed, beat together dry pudding mix and milk for 2 minutes. Gently fold in pumpkin, spice and 1/3 of whipped topping. In a dessert dish, layer half of crumbs, then half of pudding; repeat layers. Top with remaining topping; sprinkle with remaining crumbs. Cover and chill until serving time. Makes 10 to 12 servings.

Make a tray of cute pumpkin cupcakes for a Halloween
bake sale. Frost cupcakes with orange-tinted frosting and a
sprinkle of orange sanding sugar. Top each cupcake with
a small green gumdrop for a stem. So clever!

Banana Cream Pie

Caroline Pacheco
Stafford, VA

My mother and I have been making this dreamy pie since I was a young girl...it's a favorite of my father. Now I'm a mother of two little girls myself and I make it with them every Thanksgiving holiday. I hope you enjoy it as much as we do!

1/2 c. sliced almonds, toasted
   and divided
3 to 4 bananas, sliced
9-inch graham cracker pie crust
3 T. cornstarch
1/4 t. salt
1-2/3 c. water
14-oz. can sweetened
   condensed milk

3 egg yolks, beaten
2 T. margarine
1 t. vanilla extract
12-oz. container frozen whipped
   topping, thawed
Garnish: additional banana
   slices

Set aside some almonds for garnish. Line the bottom and sides of pie crust with banana slices. Sprinkle with remaining almonds; set aside. In a saucepan over medium heat, dissolve cornstarch and salt in water. Stir in condensed milk and egg yolks. Cook, stirring constantly, until thickened and bubbly, about 7 minutes. Remove from heat; stir in margarine and vanilla. Cool slightly; spoon into crust. Cover and refrigerate for at least 4 hours. At serving time, cover with whipped topping; decorate with reserved almond slices and extra banana slices. Serves 8.

Create a fall centerpiece in a snap! Hot-glue ears of mini Indian corn around a terra-cotta pot and set a vase of orange or yellow mums in the center.

Desserts

Pumpkin-Mallow Creme Pie

Cyndy DeStefano
Mercer, PA

So easy! My children are in charge of making this frozen pie for
Thanksgiving dinner...it's always a big hit at the kids' table.

15-oz. can pumpkin
7-oz. jar marshmallow creme
1/4 c. brown sugar, packed
2 t. pumpkin pie spice

12-oz. container frozen whipped
   topping, thawed and divided
9-inch graham cracker pie crust

In a large bowl, whisk together pumpkin, marshmallow creme,
brown sugar and spice. Fold in 3-1/2 cups whipped topping; return
remaining topping to refrigerator. Spoon pumpkin mixture into crust.
Cover and freeze for at least 4 hours, until firm. At serving time, let
stand at room temperature for a few minutes before cutting. Garnish
with remaining topping. Serves 8.

Slice frozen cream pies in a jiffy...let stand at room temperature
for a few minutes, then slice with a thin, sharp knife,
dipped often in hot water.

Dutch Apple Crumb Pie

Sherri Tucker Fyan
Albany, NY

This is a great apple pie! I think the crumb topping is what makes it really stand out. This pie is so popular that I can't make just one at a time, I have to make several. My husband's office co-workers even order them from me as Christmas gifts. Give it a try, I think you will agree!

8 tart apples, several different
    varieties, peeled, cored and
    sliced
1 c. brown sugar, packed and
    divided
1 to 2 t. cinnamon, to taste

9-inch pie crust
1/3 c. chilled butter
3/4 c. all-purpose flour
Garnish: whipped cream or
    ice cream

Toss together apples, 1/2 cup brown sugar and cinnamon. Place apple mixture into pie crust; set aside. In a separate large bowl, combine butter, flour and remaining brown sugar. Using a pastry cutter, work mixture into small crumbs; sprinkle over apples. Bake at 425 degrees for 10 minutes. Reduce oven to 350 degrees and bake an additional 30 to 35 minutes. Cool slightly until just warm. Serve with whipped cream or ice cream. Serves 8.

The next time a dinner guest asks, "How can I help?" be ready with an answer! Whether it's picking up a bag of ice, setting the table or even bringing a special dessert, friends are usually happy to help.

Desserts

Raw Apple Pie

Ann Dunnington
Pataskala, OH

A healthy, gluten-free, no-sugar-added dessert that can be served immediately. For a nice presentation, arrange some of the apple slices on top in a fan shape.

2-1/4 c. almonds, divided
1 t. sea salt
2-1/2 c. pitted dates, divided
1 orange, peeled and seeded
1/8 to 1/4 c. water

5 c. apples, peeled, cored and
   thinly sliced
1 c. raisins
2 T. cinnamon

Place 1/4 cup almonds into a food processor; finely chop until powdery. Sprinkle in the bottom of an ungreased 9" pie plate to coat. Process remaining almonds, sea salt and 2 cups dates to form a dough. Press into pie plate on top of almond powder. Mix together remaining dates, orange and as much water necessary to make a thick gel in the food processor. Transfer mixture to a large bowl. Add apples, raisins and cinnamon; mix well until apples are fully coated. Spoon into pie plate. Serve immediately, or refrigerate overnight. Serves 8 to 10.

Serve up a batch of skeleton cookies for Halloween! Bake a batch of your favorite gingerbread men. After the cookies are baked and cooled, add "skeletons" using white frosting and a decorator tip. So clever!

Maple Sugar-Walnut Pie

JoAnn

Luscious...a terrific use for pure maple syrup!

1 c. walnuts, coarsely chopped and toasted
9-inch pie crust, chilled
3 eggs, beaten
1 c. maple syrup

1/4 c. butter, melted and cooled slightly
2/3 c. light brown sugar, packed
1/2 t. vanilla extract
1/8 t. salt

Scatter walnuts in crust and set aside. In a bowl, whisk together remaining ingredients; pour into crust over nuts. Set pie plate on a baking sheet. Bake at 425 degrees for 10 minutes. Reduce oven to 350 degrees; bake an additional 25 to 30 minutes, until crust is golden and center is set. Cool slightly on a wire rack before serving. Serves 8.

Tennessee Fudge Pie

Dusty Jones
Paxton, IL

Mama has always made this pie for our Thanksgiving. People request it at church socials and parties too...it's a chocolate lover's dream!

2 eggs
1/2 c. butter, melted and cooled slightly
1/4 c. baking cocoa
1/4 c. all-purpose flour
1 c. sugar

2 t. vanilla extract
1/3 c. semi-sweet chocolate chips
1/3 c. broken pecan pieces
9-inch pie crust

Beat eggs slightly; stir in melted butter. Add remaining ingredients except crust; pour into unbaked crust. Bake at 350 degrees for about 25 minutes, until firm. Cool before slicing. Serves 8.

Desserts

Peanut Butter Pie

Carol Nebzydoski
Pleasant Mount, PA

My kids have always loved this creamy, peanut buttery pie. My twenty-one-year-old son even called from Texas while he was in the US Army and asked for the recipe so he could make it for his friends. They were having a small get-together before leaving for Iraq.

1/2 c. creamy or crunchy peanut
   butter
1/2 c. sugar
3-oz. pkg. cream cheese,
   softened

12-oz. container frozen whipped
   topping, thawed
9-inch graham cracker crust

In a large bowl, combine peanut butter, sugar and cream cheese; stir until well blended. Fold in whipped topping. Spoon mixture into pie crust. Cover and chill at least 2 hours before serving. Makes 6 to 8 servings.

After the kids are tucked in bed, pull out a favorite movie and enjoy a late-night dessert for two. Light some candles, start a fire in the fireplace and enjoy the evening together.

Butterscotch Pie

Cindy Neel
Gooseberry Patch

I made this old-fashioned pie for my dad's birthday...yum!
It has a really rich butterscotch flavor. Top each slice with a
generous dollop of whipped cream.

1 c. light brown sugar, packed
1/4 c. butter, softened
1/4 c. all-purpose flour
2 c. whole milk, divided

3 egg yolks, beaten
1/8 t. salt
1/2 t. vanilla extract
9-inch graham cracker crust

In a saucepan over medium-low heat, stir together brown sugar and butter until butter melts and sugar dissolves. Cook 2 to 3 minutes longer; remove from heat. In a separate bowl, mix together flour and one cup milk until smooth. Add egg yolks and salt; mix well and stir in remaining milk. Add flour mixture to brown sugar mixture in saucepan. Cook over medium-low heat until thickened, stirring constantly. Remove from heat; stir in vanilla. Spoon filling into crust; chill thoroughly. Serves 6 to 8.

Take-out boxes are available in lots of festive colors and patterns.
Keep some handy for wrapping up food gifts in a jiffy...and for
sending home dessert with party or dinner guests who
just can't eat another bite!

Scotcharoo Bars

Melisa Daniel
Alma, MI

My mom gave me this recipe for sweet, crunchy bar cookies. They're perfect for lunchboxes, party trays and just for snacking!

1 c. sugar
1 c. light corn syrup
1 c. creamy peanut butter

6 c. crispy rice cereal
1 c. semi-sweet chocolate chips
1 c. butterscotch chips

Combine sugar and corn syrup in a large heavy saucepan. Cook over medium heat, stirring often, until mixture bubbles. Remove from heat; stir in peanut butter and mix well. Add cereal; stir until well coated. Press mixture into a buttered 12"x8" baking pan; set aside. Place chocolate chips and butterscotch chips in a medium saucepan. Cook over low heat until melted; stir until well blended and smooth. Spread chocolate chip mixture over cereal mixture. Cool; cut into squares. Makes 2 dozen.

Handprint turkeys...how sweet! Have kids place their hands on rolled-out sugar cookie dough and have a grown-up cut around carefully with a table knife. After the cookies are baked and cooled, kids can add feathers, beaks and other details with tubes of frosting.

Oatmeal-Raisin Bars

Jessica Henderson
Wichita Falls, TX

*This is my husband's favorite treat. He'd love it if we always had
some on hand! It's even low in fat...what more could you ask for?*

18-1/2 oz. pkg. yellow cake mix
2 c. quick-cooking oats,
  uncooked

1/2 c. raisins
1-3/4 c. applesauce, divided
1/4 t. apple pie spice

Line the bottom and sides of a 13"x9" baking pan with aluminum foil,
allowing 2 to 3 inches to extend over sides. Lightly grease foil and set
aside. Stir together dry cake mix, oats and raisins in a large bowl. Stir
in 3/4 cup applesauce with a fork until mixture is crumbly and dry
ingredients are moistened. Press half of mixture into bottom of pan.
Stir together remaining applesauce and spice in a separate bowl;
gently spread over mixture in pan. Sprinkle with remaining cake mix
mixture. Bake at 375 degrees for 30 minutes, or until top is golden.
Cool completely in pan on a wire rack. Lift cooled bars from pan,
using foil as handles. Place on a cutting board and cut into bars.
Makes 2 dozen.

Plump up raisins and dried cranberries for baking...they'll be
soft and tasty. Cover them with boiling water and let stand
about 15 minutes, then drain well and pat dry.

Desserts

S'Mores Brownies

Abi Buening
Grand Forks, ND

These are so gooey and delicious! This is a terrific way to use up leftover Halloween candy bars, but sometimes I'll use chocolate chips instead.

18-1/2 oz. pkg. brownie mix
3 c. mini marshmallows
4 whole graham crackers,
   coarsely broken

2 chocolate candy bars, broken
   into small pieces

Prepare brownies as directed on package; bake in a greased 13"x9" baking pan. As soon as brownies are removed from oven, sprinkle with marshmallows and graham cracker crumbs. Set oven on broil. Broil for 30 to 60 seconds, until marshmallows are golden. Watch carefully, as marshmallows will brown quickly. Sprinkle with candy bar pieces. Let cool for 15 minutes before cutting into squares. Serve warm. Makes 2 dozen.

Gather pine cones to make cold-weather treats for
the birds...a fun craft for kids! Tie a hanging string to
the top of each pine cone, then spread with peanut butter
mixed with cornmeal and roll in bird seed.
The birds will love it.

Devil's Food Cookies

Lynda Robson
Boston, MA

I usually have these simple ingredients on hand, so it's really easy to whip up some yummy cookies anytime.

18-1/2 oz. pkg. devil's food
   cake mix
1/2 c. oil

2 eggs, beaten
1 c. semi-sweet chocolate chips

Mix dry cake mix and remaining ingredients. Drop by teaspoonfuls onto ungreased baking sheets. Bake at 350 degrees for 10 minutes, or until golden. Let cool on wire racks. Makes 3-1/2 dozen.

A terrific family activity for Thanksgiving weekend.
Create a gingerbread house the easy way...no baking, just fun!
Find a small house-shaped box, then turn everyone's imagination
loose with decorator frostings, assorted candies, even cereal
and pretzels! Kids love this...just be sure to have
extra candies on hand for nibbling.

Pumpkin-Chocolate Chippers

Julie Tweedie
Blaine, ME

My mom taught me this cookie recipe when I was just eight years old...she learned it from her own mother. I've been making these cookies for over forty years and now Mom calls me to ask for the recipe! They have certainly become a family favorite.

15-oz. can pumpkin
2 c. shortening
2 c. sugar
2 eggs, beaten

4 c. all-purpose flour
2 t. baking soda
2 t. cinnamon
12-oz. pkg. milk chocolate chips

In a large bowl, stir together pumpkin, shortening, sugar and eggs. Beat until well mixed. Add flour, baking soda and cinnamon. Mix well, then fold in chocolate chips. Drop onto ungreased baking sheets by teaspoonfuls. Bake at 375 degrees for 8 to 10 minutes, or until bottoms are golden. Makes about 2-1/2 dozen.

Carve an extra Jack-o'-Lantern or two and deliver to elderly neighbors so they can enjoy some Halloween fun...what a neighborly gesture!

Mini Apple Hand Pies

Sheri Dulaney
Englewood, OH

So cute in the fall!

1 Granny Smith apple, peeled,
   cored and finely chopped
1/4 c. raisins
3 T. sugar

1 t. cinnamon
12-oz. tube refrigerated biscuits
2 T. butter, diced

Combine apple, raisins, sugar and cinnamon in a bowl; toss to mix and set aside. Flatten each biscuit to a 3-inch circle. Place one tablespoon apple mixture onto each biscuit; dot with butter. Bring up sides of biscuit and pinch to seal. Place in ungreased muffin cups. Bake at 375 degrees for 11 to 13 minutes, until golden. Makes 10.

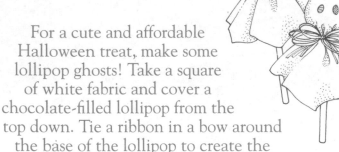

For a cute and affordable Halloween treat, make some lollipop ghosts! Take a square of white fabric and cover a chocolate-filled lollipop from the top down. Tie a ribbon in a bow around the base of the lollipop to create the ghost's head. The rest of the fabric should flow over the lollipop stick for the body. With a marker, draw two black dots on the head for the eyes. You can even use Halloween printed fabric or decorate the ghosts with stickers...let your imagination go! I learned how to make these over forty years ago in grammar school, and they still bring a smile to my face.

-Michelle Papp, Rutherford, NJ

Desserts

"Sweet Potato" Candies

Kathy Rixham
Reisterstown, MD

This recipe was given to me by my godmother a long time ago. There's no actual sweet potato in these candies...instead, they're shaped to look like little sweet potatoes. During the Depression, my godmother sold these candies at church bazaars. She raised enough money that way to buy a new refrigerator!

1 c. butter
8 t. vanilla extract
2 t. salt
8 lbs. powdered sugar

20-oz. pkg. sweetened flaked
   coconut
1 c. milk, warmed
Garnish: cinnamon

Soften butter until almost melted. Mix together butter, vanilla and salt in a very large bowl. Stir in powdered sugar and coconut; mixture will be lumpy. Knead until smooth, adding milk a little at a time. Break off one-inch balls and roll into sweet potato shapes. Roll candies in cinnamon to coat. Place in a covered container; keep refrigerated. Makes about 14 to 15 dozen.

Homemade candy is always a welcome gift! Make the gift even sweeter...place individual candies in mini paper muffin cups and arrange in a decorated box.

Dulce de Leche Bars

Andrea Heyart
Aubrey, TX

This rich chocolate and caramel dessert makes a wonderful take-along to cookie exchanges and holiday parties! Dulce de leche is caramelized sweetened condensed milk...you'll find it in the Hispanic aisle or with the dessert toppings.

18-1/2 oz. pkg. spice cake mix
2 eggs, beaten
1/3 c. unsweetened applesauce
6-oz. pkg. semi-sweet chocolate chips

14-oz. can dulce de leche
1/4 c. butter

In a bowl, combine dry cake mix, eggs and applesauce. Stir until mixture forms a sticky dough. In a 13"x9" baking pan, spread and pat down 3/4 of mixture; set aside. Place chocolate chips, dulce de leche and butter in a microwave-safe bowl. Microwave on high for one to 2 minutes, until melted. Stir well to combine; spread over first layer. Place large spoonfuls of remaining cake mix mixture on top, flattening and spreading as much as possible. Bake at 350 degrees for 20 to 25 minutes, until golden. Cool completely before cutting into bars. Makes 10 to 14.

Invite a young friend to bake with you. Whether you're a basic baker or a master chef, you're sure to have fun as you measure, stir and sample together.

Slow Cooker

Off Low High

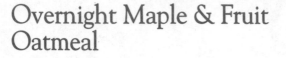

Overnight Maple & Fruit Oatmeal

Kristen DeSimone
Peabody, MA

My husband and I are big oatmeal fans! As soon as the chill of fall creeps in, this is one of our favorite breakfasts to enjoy. I like to use a plastic slow-cooker liner for easy clean-up.

2 c. milk
1/4 c. maple syrup
1 T. butter, sliced
1 c. long-cooking oats, uncooked
1/2 c. raisins
1 c. apple, peeled, cored and chopped
1/2 c. chopped walnuts or pecans
1/2 t. cinnamon
1/8 t. salt

The night before, combine all ingredients in a slow cooker and mix well. Cover and cook on low setting overnight for 8 to 9 hours. Stir before serving. Serves 8.

Hosting a game-day or holiday brunch? Use a slow cooker set on low to keep sausage gravy, scrambled eggs or other breakfast foods warm and toasty.

Slow Cooker

Apple Breakfast Cobbler

Debbie Martinez
West Valley City, UT

My grandkids love eating breakfast when they help make it!
Together we assemble this the night before. The kids wake up to
a wonderful aroma and they're so proud they did the cooking.

4 apples, peeled, cored and
   sliced
1/4 c. honey
2 T. butter, melted

1 t. cinnamon
2 c. granola cereal
Garnish: sugar, milk

The night before, place apples into a slow cooker sprayed with
non-stick vegetable spray. Stir together honey, butter, cinnamon and
granola; add to slow cooker. Cover and cook on low setting overnight
for 7 to 9 hours. Serve topped with sugar and milk. Serves 4.

A touch of whimsy...use Grandma's old cow-shaped
pitcher to serve milk or cream for breakfast cereal,
oatmeal and coffee.

All-in-One Sunrise Casserole

Jessica Robertson
Fishers, IN

Equally delicious made with crisply cooked bacon or cubed baked ham instead of sausage. Add a simple fruit cup and breakfast is ready to go!

32-oz. pkg. frozen shredded
   hashbrowns
1 lb. ground turkey breakfast
   sausage links or patties,
   browned and drained
1 onion, diced
1 green pepper, diced

1-1/2 c. shredded Cheddar
   cheese
1 doz. eggs, beaten
1 c. milk
1 t. salt
1 t. pepper

The night before, place a layer of hashbrowns in the bottom of a slow cooker, followed by a layer of sausage, then onion, green pepper and cheese. Repeat layering 2 to 3 more times, ending with cheese on top. Whisk together eggs, milk, salt and pepper; pour over layers in slow cooker. Cover and cook on low setting overnight for 10 to 12 hours. Makes 6 to 8 servings.

What a neighborly gesture...invite the family of your child's new school friend for a weekend brunch. Send them home with a basket filled with maps and coupons to local shops and attractions.

Slow Cooker

Creamy Crock Hashbrowns

Diane Cohen
The Woodlands, TX

I like to serve this yummy side with grilled ham slices. The recipe can easily be halved for a smaller group...but don't underestimate how many people will ask for seconds!

32-oz. pkg. frozen diced
   potatoes
2 c. sour cream
10-3/4 oz. can cream of celery
   soup
10-3/4 oz. can cream of chicken
   soup

1 onion, chopped
1/4 c. margarine, melted
1/4 t. pepper
2 c. shredded Cheddar cheese

Place potatoes in a slow cooker. Combine remaining ingredients; pour over potatoes. Stir to mix well. Cover and cook on low setting for 4 to 5 hours, or high setting for 3 hours. Makes 10 to 12 servings.

Vintage-style postcards make terrific fall decorations. Tuck them between gourds and mini pumpkins on the mantel or make color copies and secure around a canning jar candle. Just tie on a tag for a clever hostess gift.

Parmesan Biscuit Bread

Vickie

Nothing says comfort like warm, fresh-baked bread, and what could be easier than putting your slow cooker to work for you?

1-1/2 c. biscuit baking mix
2 egg whites, beaten
1/2 c. milk
1 T. dried, minced onion

1 T. sugar
1-1/2 t. garlic powder
1/4 c. grated Parmesan cheese

In a bowl, combine all ingredients except Parmesan cheese. Stir until dough forms. Spray a 2-1/2 to 3-quart slow cooker generously with non-stick vegetable spray. Spoon dough into slow cooker; sprinkle with cheese. Cover and cook on high setting for one to 1-1/4 hours. Cut into wedges to serve. Makes one loaf.

Fill clear vases with candy corn, then slip a fanciful half-mask onto each vase. Line up two or three for a speedy, spooky centerpiece.

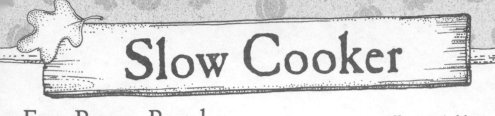
Easy Brown Bread

Tiffany Brinkley
Broomfield, CO

This hearty old-fashioned bread is best hot from the slow cooker,
topped with lots of creamery butter. Mmm!

2 c. whole-wheat flour
1 c. all-purpose flour
1 T. baking powder
1 t. salt

2 T. molasses
2 T. oil
1-1/3 c. water

Stir together flours, baking powder and salt in a large bowl. Add
remaining ingredients; mix until moistened. Turn into a greased
5-quart slow cooker. Place 5 paper towels on top of slow cooker to
catch any condensation. Add lid; place a wooden toothpick between
paper towels and lid so a little steam can escape. Cook on high setting
for 2 hours; do not uncover while cooking. Loosen sides of bread with
a knife; turn out onto a wire rack. Makes one loaf.

Soups and stews are so tasty served with warm bread. Top each
slice with the prettiest butter pats...simply use a tiny cookie
cutter to shape chilled butter slices.

Nana's Crockery Meatballs

Stephanie Norton
Saginaw, TX

These meatballs have been famous for generations and begged for at parties by young & old alike.

2-1/2 c. catsup
1 c. brown sugar, packed
2 T. Worcestershire sauce

2 lbs. ground beef chuck
1.35-oz. pkg. onion soup mix
5-oz. can evaporated milk

Stir together catsup, brown sugar and Worcestershire sauce in a slow cooker; cover. Turn slow cooker to high setting and allow mixture to warm while preparing meatballs. Combine remaining ingredients; mix well and form into one-inch balls. Place meatballs on an ungreased rimmed baking sheet. Bake at 325 degrees for 20 minutes; drain. Transfer meatballs to slow cooker. Turn slow cooker to low setting. Cover and cook for 2 to 3 hours, stirring gently halfway through. Makes 4 dozen.

My three kids and I love Halloween! We've started our own tradition...every Friday night in October, we have a pizza & movie night. We make a pizza (or order one) and watch a Halloween movie together. Our favorite movies are my old black & white ones: *Dracula, Frankenstein, The Wolfman* and *The Mummy*! These spooky characters bring back such great Halloween memories from when I was young.

-Melinda Magness, Hodgen, OK

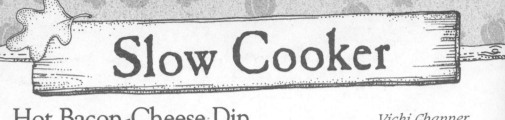

Slow Cooker

Hot Bacon-Cheese Dip

Vicki Channer
Fairview Heights, IL

Recently a group of our friends got together for a "Bacon Blast"!
Yes, all of the food from appetizers to dessert was made with bacon.
It was great fun...why not throw a Bacon Blast of your own?

2 8-oz. pkgs. cream cheese,
   cubed
4 c. shredded Cheddar cheese
1 to 2 c. half-and-half
2 t. Worcestershire sauce
1 t. dried, minced onion

1 t. mustard
1 lb. bacon, crisply cooked and
   crumbled
tortilla chips or French bread
   slices

In a 1-1/2 quart slow cooker, combine all ingredients except bacon,
tortilla chips and bread. Cover and cook on low setting for 2 hours, or
until cheeses are melted, stirring occasionally. Just before serving, stir
in bacon. Serve warm with tortilla chips or bread. Makes 4 cups.

Make it easy for guests to mingle and chat...set up food at
several tables instead of one big party buffet. Place hot foods
on one table, chilled foods at another, sweets and
beverages at yet another.

Cranberry Wild Rice

Judith Jennings
Ironwood, MI

This recipe is a favorite to make when the frost is on the pumpkin!
It warms and delights one's senses...a true comfort food.

1-1/2 c. wild rice, uncooked
2 14-oz. cans vegetable broth
4-1/2 oz. jar sliced mushrooms
4 green onions, sliced
1 T. butter, melted

1/2 t. salt
1/4 t. pepper
1/2 c. slivered almonds, toasted
1/3 c. sweetened dried
   cranberries

In a 2 to 3-1/2 quart slow cooker, mix together all ingredients except nuts and berries. Cover and cook on low setting for 4 to 5 hours, until wild rice is tender. Stir nuts and berries into rice mixture. Cover and cook on low setting an additional 15 minutes before serving. Serves 6.

Toasting really brings out the flavor of shelled nuts...and it's easy. Place nuts in a small dry skillet. Cook and stir over low heat for a few minutes, until toasty and golden...it's that simple!

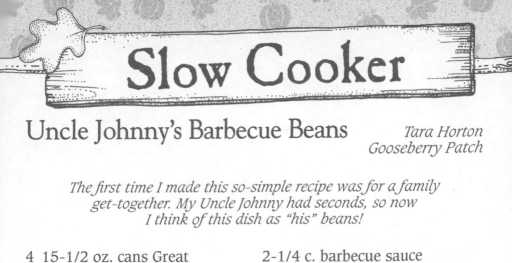

Slow Cooker

Uncle Johnny's Barbecue Beans

Tara Horton
Gooseberry Patch

*The first time I made this so-simple recipe was for a family
get-together. My Uncle Johnny had seconds, so now
I think of this dish as "his" beans!*

4 15-1/2 oz. cans Great
   Northern beans, drained
4 15-1/2 oz. cans black beans,
   drained
2 15-oz. cans butter beans,
   drained

2-1/4 c. barbecue sauce
2-1/4 c. salsa
3/4 c. brown sugar, packed
1 t. hot pepper sauce

Combine all ingredients in a slow cooker; stir to mix. Cover and cook
on low setting for 2 hours. Makes 16 servings.

Oh-so clever! Alongside each slow cooker,
use wooden alphabet tiles to spell out recipe names.
Guests will know just what's inside and it's
a fun twist on the traditional table tent.

Cinnamon-Glazed Carrots

Julie Ann Perkins
Anderson, IN

*Use your slow cooker to free up needed stove space and turn an
ordinary dish into a scrumptious side...guests of all ages will dig in!*

2 lbs. baby carrots
3/4 c. brown sugar, packed
1/4 c. honey
1/2 c. orange juice

2 T. butter, melted
3/4 to 1 t. cinnamon
Garnish: orange zest

Place carrots in a 4-quart slow cooker coated with non-stick vegetable
spray. Combine remaining ingredients except zest in a bowl; pour over
carrots and toss until well-coated. Cover and cook on low setting for
3 to 4 hours, until tender, stirring twice during cooking time. Transfer
carrots in a serving dish and cover to keep warm. Pour sauce from
slow cooker into a small saucepan. Cook over medium heat until
sauce is reduced by half, stirring frequently. Pour sauce over carrots;
toss to coat. Garnish with orange zest. Serves 6 to 8.

Set a packet of pumpkin seeds at each place setting for a fun,
colorful favor...check end-of-summer sales for bargains.
Garden seeds are usually good for at least a year,
so guests can save them to plant in next year's garden.

Slow Cooker

Peachy-Keen Sweet Taters

Cathi Carpenter
Marietta, GA

I make these sweet potatoes for every holiday...it's the only way our eight-year-old son will eat them! Try this dish with apple pie filling too, substituting apple pie spice for the ginger. Yummy!

2-1/4 c. sweet potatoes, peeled
   and cubed
21-oz. can peach pie filling
2 T. butter, melted
1 t. fresh ginger, peeled and
   grated, or 1 t. ground ginger

1/4 t. salt
2 T. brown sugar, packed
1/8 t. cinnamon
1/2 c. pecans, coarsely chopped

Place sweet potatoes in a 4-quart slow cooker sprayed with non-stick vegetable spray. Add pie filling, butter, ginger and salt; mix well to coat. Cover and cook on high setting for 2-1/2 to 3 hours. In a small saucepan over medium-low heat, combine remaining ingredients. Heat until glazed and bubbly, stirring frequently. Spoon pecans onto an aluminum foil-lined baking sheet to cool. Just before serving, gently stir potatoes; sprinkle with pecans. Serves 6.

Hosting a Thanksgiving dinner
with all the trimmings?
With a slow cooker, you can
free up oven space by preparing
a savory slow-cooked side dish.
Slow cookers are so handy,
you may want more than one!

French Broccoli-Rice Soup

Annette Ingram
Grand Rapids, MI

My family likes to warm up with mugs of this creamy soup after we've spent a chilly afternoon raking leaves. Top with dollops of sour cream and a sprinkle of parsley for a special touch.

10-3/4 oz. can cream of
   mushroom soup
12-oz. can evaporated milk
1-1/2 c. hot water
2 c. frozen chopped broccoli,
   thawed

3/4 c. shredded Cheddar cheese
1/2 c. carrots, peeled and diced
   or grated
1/2 c. onion, diced
1/3 c. instant rice, uncooked
1 t. dried parsley

In a bowl, stir together soup, evaporated milk and water until blended. Add remaining ingredients and mix well. Transfer to a slow cooker coated with butter-flavored vegetable spray. Cover and cook on low setting for 3 to 4 hours. Stir again before serving. Makes 4 to 6 servings.

Top bowls of hot soup with popcorn or tiny pretzels instead of croutons for a crunchy surprise.

Slow Cooker

French Onion Soup

Lori Rosenberg
University Heights, OH

When I was a kid, French onion soup was always a special treat...it seemed so grown-up! With the slow cooker, I can enjoy this treat more often as an adult.

3 onions, sliced
3 T. margarine, melted
3 T. all-purpose flour
1 T. Worcestershire sauce

1/4 t. sugar
pepper to taste
4 14-1/2 oz. cans beef broth

Mix together onions and margarine in a 3-1/2 to 6-quart slow cooker. Cover and cook on high setting for 30 to 35 minutes, until onions begin to turn slightly golden around edges. Blend together flour, Worcestershire sauce, sugar and pepper. Stir flour mixture and broth into onions. Cover and cook on low setting for 7 to 9 hours, until onions are very tender. Ladle into soup bowls. Top each bowl with a slice of Cheesy Broiled French Bread. Serves 8.

Cheesy Broiled French Bread:

3/4 c. shredded mozzarella
    cheese
1/4 c. shredded Parmesan
    cheese

8 slices French bread, one-inch
    thick

Mix cheeses together; place an equal amount of mixture on each slice of bread. Place bread on a broiler pan. Broil for one to 2 minutes, or until cheese starts to melt.

Keep frozen chopped onions, peppers and veggie blends on hand for quick slow-cooker meal prep. They'll thaw quickly so you can toss together a recipe in a snap...no peeling, chopping or dicing!

Chile Verde Soup

Lisa Sett
Thousand Oaks, CA

Hearty, filling and goes together in a hurry!

1/2 lb. pork tenderloin, cut
   into 1/2-inch cubes
1 t. oil
2 c. chicken broth
2 15-oz. cans white beans,
   drained and rinsed

2 4-oz. cans diced green chiles
1/4 t. ground cumin
1/4 t. dried oregano
salt and pepper to taste
6 to 8 sprigs fresh cilantro

In a skillet over medium heat, cook pork in oil for one to 2 minutes, until browned. Place pork in a slow cooker. Add remaining ingredients; stir. Cover and cook on low setting for 4 to 6 hours. Serves 6 to 8.

A fun new way to serve cornbread...mix up the batter, thin slightly with a little extra milk, then bake until crisp in a waffle iron. Perfect with chili!

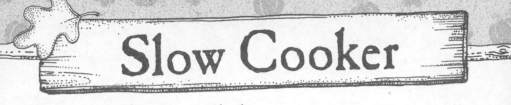

Slow Cooker

Krysti's Delicious Chili

*Krysti Hilfiger
Covington, PA*

*This chili is always on hand at the Apple Cider Weekend we have
in October. Made in a slow cooker...what could be easier?*

1 lb. ground beef, browned and
   drained
2 28-oz. cans crushed tomatoes
2 15-1/2 oz. cans light red
   kidney beans

3 T. dried, minced onion
1 T. chili powder
1 T. sugar or to taste
salt and pepper to taste

Place all ingredients in a slow cooker. Cover and cook on high setting
for 4 hours. Serves 6.

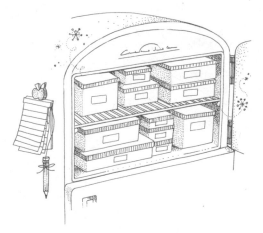

How comforting to have a freezer full of delicious soup! Use an
extra-large slow cooker (or two regular size) to make a double
batch of a favorite slow-cooker soup recipe. Freeze half for later
in a freezer-safe container. To serve, thaw the soup overnight
the fridge and heat 'til bubbly in a saucepan on the stove.

No-Fuss Turkey Breast

Amy Hunt
Traphill, NC

My sister fixes turkey this way for an easy
"Thanksgiving" meal all year 'round.

5 to 6-lb. boneless turkey breast   1/4 c. margarine, sliced
3 c. water   1/2 t. salt-free herb seasoning

Place turkey breast in a large slow cooker. Add water, margarine and seasoning salt. Cover and cook on low setting for 7 to 8 hours, until juices run clear when pierced and a meat thermometer inserted in thickest part reads 170 degrees. Remove to a serving platter. Cover and let stand 5 to 10 minutes before slicing. Serves 8 to 10.

On Thanksgiving Day in 1953, I was nearly ten years old. I loved Thanksgiving and all the fun of helping Mom prepare our favorite foods. Our relatives lived many miles away so we seldom saw them, especially during the winter months. As dinnertime drew near, I went outside and waited. The air was filled with a misty fog so I couldn't see too far down the road. It was getting late and I was fearful they had lost their way. As I peered through the fog, I saw a figure walking...as he got closer, I realized it was my Uncle Maynard in his Army uniform. I flew down the road and into his arms. He had served in the Korean War and came to have Thanksgiving dinner with us before going home to North Dakota. We celebrated with a generous table filled with wonderful food, thankful for having Uncle Maynard back, safe from harm's way.

-Karen Overholt, Kennewick, WA

Slow Cooker

Cherry-Pecan Stuffed Turkey

Shirl Parsons
Cape Carteret, NC

This flavorful recipe came from a cookbook Mom gave me years ago...this was one of her favorites. It's delicious made with dried cherries and apricot preserves too, so feel free to substitute!

3 to 4-lb. boneless turkey breast
2 c. cooked rice
1/3 c. sweetened dried cherries
1/3 c. chopped pecans

1 t. poultry seasoning
1/4 c. peach preserves
1 t. Worcestershire sauce

Remove and discard skin from turkey breast. With a sharp knife, slice 3/4 of the way through turkey at one-inch intervals. Stir together rice, cherries, pecans and seasoning in a large bowl. Stuff rice mixture between slices. Insert skewers lengthwise in turkey to hold it together, if needed; place in a large slow cooker. Cover and cook on low setting 5 to 6 hours, until juices run clear when pierced and a meat thermometer inserted in thickest part reads 170 degrees. Stir together preserves and Worcestershire sauce; spoon over turkey. Cover and let stand for 5 minutes before serving. Serves 6 to 8.

Tired of turkey sandwiches after Thanksgiving? For a completely different taste, make turkey quesadillas! Sprinkle a flour tortilla with chopped turkey, shredded cheese and any other add-ins you like. Top with another tortilla and cook in a lightly greased skillet until cheese melts, turning once. Cut into wedges and serve with salsa. Yum!

Autumn Cranberry Chicken

Kim Jewett
Highland, UT

*A favorite autumn meal at our house...it's speedy for busy days
and the cranberries remind us of the holidays to come.*

4 boneless, skinless chicken
   breasts
16-oz. can whole-berry
   cranberry sauce

1 c. Russian salad dressing
1.35-oz. pkg. onion soup mix
cooked rice

Place chicken in a slow cooker, cutting pieces in half if desired.
Combine remaining ingredients except rice; spoon over chicken. Cover
and cook on low setting for 6 hours, or until chicken juices run clear
when pierced. Serve over cooked rice. Serves 4.

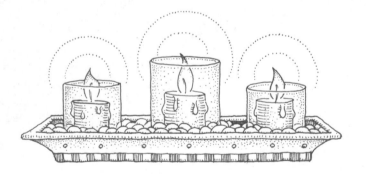

Set lighted votives on a shallow tray filled with
glass pebbles for a quick & easy centerpiece.

Slow Cooker

Curried Harvest Chicken

Jill Ball
Highland, UT

My family loves meat combined with fruit, so this savory dish is a favorite. I can toss it together in the morning and then forget about it until it's time for dinner. Tasty and convenient!

6 boneless, skinless chicken
   breasts
12-oz. pkg. frozen mixed
   vegetables
21-oz. can apple pie filling

2 10-3/4 oz. cans cream of
   mushroom soup
2 to 3 T. curry powder
1 t. salt

Combine all ingredients in a large slow cooker; stir to mix. Cover and cook on low setting for 6 hours, or until chicken juices run clear when pierced. Serves 6.

Bring out Mom's vintage Thanksgiving china early to
get into the mood for fall. Use the bowls for soup suppers,
the teacups for dessert get-togethers and even layer
sandwich fixin's on the turkey platter!

Laura's Chicken & Noodles

Laura Justice
Indianapolis, IN

Comfort food made easy.

4 boneless, skinless chicken
   breasts
salt and pepper to taste
2 10-3/4 oz. cans cream of
   chicken soup

14-oz. can chicken broth
12-oz. pkg. medium egg
   noodles, cooked

Sprinkle chicken with salt and pepper; place in a slow cooker. Spoon
soup over chicken. Cover and cook on low setting for 6 hours, or until
chicken juices run clear and chicken falls apart. Remove chicken and
shred; return to soup mixture in slow cooker. Add broth and cooked
noodles; mix well. Cover and cook on low setting for an additional
30 minutes, or until heated through. Serves 6.

Fill a basket with everything that's needed for
a simple supper like Laura's Chicken & Noodles
and deliver to new parents...how thoughtful!

Slow Cooker

Heavenly Beef Brisket

Kim AhMu
Independence, MO

An easy dinner for Sunday after church...it's a family favorite!
We enjoy this scrumptious brisket with either potatoes or rice, topped
with gravy made from the delicious juices in the slow cooker.

1 lb. carrots, peeled
Optional: 1 onion, sliced and
   divided
5 to 6-lb. beef brisket, trimmed

salt, pepper, onion powder and
   garlic powder to taste
1 c. water

Place carrots in a single layer on a large piece of heavy-duty
aluminum foil. Top with half of onion slices, if desired. Sprinkle brisket
on both sides with salt, pepper, onion powder and garlic powder. Place
brisket on top of carrots. If necessary, cut brisket in half to fit in your
slow cooker; layer the halves on top of each other. Place remaining
onion slices on top, if using. Lay another piece of foil on top; fold
edges to seal tight. Pour water into a large slow cooker; add foil packet.
Cover and cook for 8 hours on low setting, or 4 to 5 hours on high
setting. Serves 4 to 6.

Turn leftover roast beef or chicken into a country-style pot pie.
Cube meat and add a can or two of mixed veggies, a can of
cream soup and seasonings to taste. Combine in a slow cooker;
cover and cook on low setting for 4 to 6 hours. Top with
refrigerated biscuits 30 minutes before serving time, cover and
cook on low until biscuits are done. Mmm!

Apple-Spice Country Ribs

Tammi Miller
Attleboro, MA

One fall weekend after apple picking, I tossed together this recipe. I was trying to work apples into everything I could think of to use them up, and used some of the last ones in this recipe. Once it was done, I wished I'd made it first so I could make it again!

2 to 3 lbs. country pork ribs
3 baking apples, cored and cut
   into wedges
2/3 c. apple cider
1 onion, thinly sliced

1 t. cinnamon
1 t. allspice
1/2 t. salt
1/4 t. pepper
cooked rice or mashed potatoes

If bone-in ribs are used, slice into serving-size portions. Place all ingredients except rice or potatoes in a slow cooker; stir to coat. Cover and cook on low setting for 7 to 9 hours. Juices will thicken as they cool; stir if separated. Serve over hot cooked rice or mashed potatoes. Serves 4 to 6.

Try a new side dish instead of rice or noodles...barley pilaf.
Simply prepare quick-cooking barley with chicken broth,
seasoned with a little chopped onion and dried parsley.
Filling, quick and tasty!

n/a

6-Bean Casserole

Andrea Royer-James
Indiana, PA

I remember my mom making this hearty dish for large gatherings when I was a child. It was my favorite then and today, even after a few small additions, it's still a favorite of mine!

1/2 to 1 lb. ground beef,
  browned and drained
1/2 lb. bacon, crisply cooked
  and crumbled
15-oz. can green beans
15-oz. can yellow wax beans
15-oz. can butter beans
15-oz. can Great Northern beans
16-oz. can light red kidney
  beans

16-oz. can pork & beans
1/2 c. catsup
1/2 c. onion, chopped
3/4 c. brown sugar, packed
1/2 c. sugar
2 t. white vinegar
1 t. dry mustard
1 t. salt

Lightly grease the top edge of a 5-quart slow cooker. Add beef and bacon; set aside. Drain all beans except pork & beans; place in a large bowl. Add undrained pork & beans to bowl; stir gently and add to slow cooker. Mix together remaining ingredients; add to slow cooker and stir gently. Cover and cook on high setting for 2 to 3 hours. Serves 8 to 10.

Make it a one-pot meal...add some veggies to a favorite slow-cooker recipe. Potatoes, carrots and onions should be placed in the bottom and along the sides of a slow cooker, with the meat on top, as they generally take longer to cook.

Saucy BBQ Pork Tenderloin

Gina Filippelli
Taylors, SC

My son and I came up with this recipe together...it's tasty served on rolls or enjoyed all by itself. Just add French fries or crispy golden potato puffs for a meal everyone will love.

2 to 3-lb. pork tenderloin,
  trimmed
salt and pepper to taste
3 c. water

18-oz. bottle barbecue sauce,
  divided
Optional: 12-oz. pkg. Kaiser
  rolls, split

Place pork in a slow cooker; season with salt and pepper. Pour water over pork. Cover and cook on high setting for about 5 hours. Pour off half of remaining liquid in slow cooker; add 3/4 of barbecue sauce. Cover and cook on high setting for one additional hour. Reduce setting to low; cook for one additional hour, or until pork is very tender and falls apart. Serve on Kaiser rolls, if desired, accompanied by remaining barbecue sauce. Serves 4 to 6.

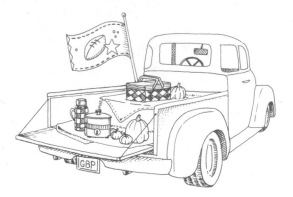

Tailgate in style...fly a family flag over your tailgating spot so it's easy for friends & family to find you. Cut a length of fabric, then let the little ones get creative with fabric paint and glitter glue. A one-of-a-kind creation!

Slow Cooker

Shredded Pork Sandwiches

JonCarole Gilbreath
Tyler, TX

Everyone will love these savory, smoky sandwiches. They're simple to fix, but that's your little secret!

3 to 4 thick-sliced boneless
   pork chops
1 onion, sliced
1 tomato, chopped
4-oz. can sliced mushrooms,
   drained

2 t. chipotle seasoning
1/2 c. barbecue sauce
1/4 c. brown sugar, packed
1/2 t. salt
8 whole-wheat buns, split

Place pork chops in a slow cooker; top with onion, tomato and mushrooms. Stir chipotle seasoning into barbecue sauce and spoon over pork chops. Cover and cook on high setting for one hour. Reduce to low setting and cook for about 8 hours, until very tender. Remove pork chops and shred with a fork; set aside. Pour juices and vegetables from slow cooker into a saucepan; stir in brown sugar and salt. Bring to a boil; simmer for several minutes, until reduced slightly. Stir in shredded pork; heat through. Serve on buns. Serves 6 to 8.

Warm sandwich buns for a crowd...easy! Fill a roaster with buns, cover with heavy-duty aluminum foil and cut several slits in the foil. Top with several dampened paper towels and tightly cover with more foil. Place in a 250-degree oven for 20 minutes. Rolls will be hot and steamy.

Mom's Swiss Steak

JoAnna Lovin-Marsh
Vadnais Heights, MN

*A favorite memory from my childhood...coming home from school
on a crisp fall day to the wonderful rich aroma of this dish.
True comfort food.*

2 lbs. beef round steak, cut into
   serving-size portions
1 c. water
1.35-oz. pkg. onion soup mix
2 10-3/4 oz. cans cream of
   mushroom soup

4-1/2 oz. can sliced mushrooms,
   drained
mashed potatoes

Place beef in a slow cooker sprayed with non-stick vegetable spray.
Add water; sprinkle soup mix over beef. Top with soup and
mushrooms. Cover and cook on low setting for 7 to 8 hours, until beef
is tender. Serve portions with hot mashed potatoes, topped with gravy
from slow cooker. Serves 6 to 8.

Create mini recipe cards listing the ingredients of favorite
one-dish dinners. Glue a button magnet on the back and
place on the fridge...so handy whenever it's time to
make out a shopping list!

Slow Cooker

Pepperoncini Beef Buns

Ellen Smith
College Station, TX

This is simply the easiest slow-cooker recipe I have...it's awesome!

3-1/2 to 4-lb. beef chuck roast
16-oz. jar pepperoncini

6 to 8 sandwich buns, split

Place roast in a large slow cooker. Pour pepperoncini with juice over roast. Cover and cook for 8 to 10 hours on low setting. Shred beef and serve on buns. Serves 6 to 8.

Start a new tradition...a no-fuss night-before-Thanksgiving supper from the slow cooker! Whether it's chili, shredded meat sandwiches or another favorite, fill up the slow cooker Wednesday morning and then sit down that night to a family meal together. You'll be giving yourself a few peaceful moments to reflect on your blessings before all the hustle & bustle of Thanksgiving Day begins.

Triple Vanilla Delight

Linda Molloy
Syracuse, NY

*I adapted this recipe from a chocolate version that appeared in a previous **Gooseberry Patch** cookbook. My grandkids are very fond of both versions!*

18-1/2 oz. pkg. white cake mix
3.4-oz. pkg. instant vanilla
   pudding mix
3 eggs, beaten
1 c. oil

1 c. water
6-oz. pkg. white chocolate chips
Garnish: vanilla ice cream or
   whipped cream

Mix together dry cake mix, dry pudding mix and remaining ingredients except garnish. Spoon into a greased large slow cooker. Cover and cook on high setting for about 5 hours, until set. Serve warm, topped with ice cream or whipped cream. Makes 8 to 12 servings.

Dollop fresh whipped cream on warm slow-cooker desserts...irresistible! Pour a pint of whipping cream into a deep, narrow bowl. Beat with an electric mixer on medium speed, gradually increasing to high speed. When soft peaks form, add sugar to taste.

Slow Cooker

Simmered Autumn Applesauce

Jennifer Levy
Warners, NY

*The kids will love this recipe! It's perfect for the apples
you picked together at the orchard. Let the delicious aroma
fill your kitchen on a crisp fall day.*

8 apples, several different
    varieties, peeled, cored and
    cubed
1 c. water

1/2 c. brown sugar, packed
1 t. cinnamon
1/2 t. pumpkin pie spice

Add all ingredients to a slow cooker; stir. Cover and cook on low
setting for 6 to 8 hours. Mash apples with the back of a spoon; stir
again. Let cool slightly before serving. Makes 6 servings.

Homemade caramel apple dip...yum! Spray a slow cooker with
non-stick vegetable spray and pour in two cans of sweetened
condensed milk. Cover and cook on low setting for 2-1/2 hours,
until milk thickens; stir. Cover and continue cooking another
one to 1-1/2 hours, stirring every 15 minutes, until thick and
golden. Serve warm or chilled; store in the refrigerator.

Incredibly Yummy Pumpkin Cake

Renee Ortiz
Windsor, CA

I came up with this dessert recipe to avoid rolling out a pie crust and my family is oh-so-thankful. It has all the flavor of a pumpkin pie, but served up warm...it's extreme comfort food!

1/2 c. butter, melted and divided
18-1/2 oz. pkg. yellow cake mix
29-oz. can pumpkin
2 eggs, beaten

12-oz. can evaporated milk
1 T. cinnamon
1 T. allspice
Garnish: whipped cream

Pour 1/4 cup melted butter into a slow cooker; use some of it to grease the sides. Dump in dry cake mix. Add remaining butter and other ingredients except garnish; stir. Cover and cook on low setting for about 2 hours, until set. Serve warm, topped with whipped cream. Makes 8 to 12 servings.

Cooked, mashed pumpkin, butternut squash and sweet potatoes can be used interchangeably in quick breads, pies, soups and other everyday dishes. Try a different combination and discover a whole new taste!

Slow Cooker

Chocolate Pudding Cake

Lena Butler Smith
Pickerington, OH

My family doesn't have a lot of free time because of work, school, sports and everything else. There's usually no time for dessert...at times, we're lucky to get a good dinner! With this scrumptious recipe, dessert is already made when we get home. My three kids love it...it's a hit with church groups and at parties too!

18-1/2 oz. pkg. chocolate
    cake mix
3.9-oz. pkg. instant chocolate
    pudding mix
1 pt. sour cream
4 eggs, beaten

3/4 c. oil
1 c. water
6-oz. pkg. semi-sweet chocolate
    chips
Optional: vanilla ice cream

In a large bowl, stir together dry mixes and remaining ingredients except ice cream. Pour into a large slow cooker sprayed with non-stick vegetable spray. Cover and cook on low setting for 5 to 7 hours. Do not stir while cooking! When done, dessert should be cake-like with some chocolate "lava" in the center. Serve warm, over ice cream if desired. Makes 6 to 8 servings.

A candy wreath is a sweet treat...and there's no trick to making it! Tie a variety of wrapped candies onto a wire wreath form with short lengths of ribbon. Look for old-fashioned candies in fall colors like root beer barrels and butterscotch candies. Continue to tie on candy until you cover the entire wreath, then tie on a big ribbon bow and a small scissors for snipping off pieces.

Chocolatey Peanut Drops

Patty Fosnight
Wildorado, TX

We've been making this scrumptious candy for years now. One of the easiest-ever candies to make and still a favorite of all! Ribbon-tied icing cones of this candy make a great hostess gift.

16-oz. jar lightly salted peanuts
16-oz. jar unsalted dry-roasted
  peanuts
12-oz. pkg. semi-sweet
  chocolate chips

12-oz. pkg. white chocolate
  chips
1 lb. melting chocolate, chopped
12-oz. pkg. toffee baking bits

Place all ingredients into a slow cooker sprayed with non-stick vegetable spray. Cover and cook on low setting for 2 hours. Stir until smooth and well blended. Drop by teaspoonfuls onto wax paper; let stand until cool. Makes 6 dozen pieces.

For your favorite college student who's away from home, a care package of sweets is a terrific surprise! Along with baked goodies or homemade candy, tuck in a phone card and some family photos.

Slow Cooker

Peanut Butter-Caramel Apples

Barbara Bargdill
Gooseberry Patch

*We go apple picking every fall and I love cooking apples in my
slow cooker. This recipe is just plain yummy!*

12-oz. jar caramel ice cream
   topping
1/2 c. creamy peanut butter
1/2 c. water
2-1/2 lbs. Fuji apples, peeled,
   cored and sliced into
   1/2-inch thick wedges

Garnish: vanilla ice cream
Optional: chopped peanuts

Coat a slow cooker with non-stick vegetable spray. Add caramel
topping, peanut butter and water; whisk until smooth. Add apples; stir
to coat. Cover and cook on low setting for 3 to 4 hours. Serve topped
with ice cream. Sprinkle with chopped peanuts, if desired. Serves
about 8.

My earliest autumn memories...crunching through brilliantly
colored leaves, ringlets of fireplace smoke circling the chimneys
and oh, the parties to celebrate it all! Halloween parties with
orange and black streamers hung throughout, nut cups and party
frills, black cats and big yellow moons...all fanciful but not too
scary! The tricks were apple bobbing and cake walks, musical
chairs and costume contests...the treats were homemade caramel
corn, candied apples, spiced doughnuts and warm apple cider.
I remember floating home after these parties in a flurry of golden
glitter and bright orange ribbon, clutching my sack of treats
and eagerly looking forward to all the other parties
that would celebrate the season.

-Suzie Kekauoha, Visalia, CA

Tiffani's Hot Spiced Cider

Tiffani Schulte
Wyandotte, MI

I've been making this delicious, soul-warming brew ever since my teenagers were babies...for church coffee hours, homeroom mom teas, PTO events, baby showers and just for fun. It smells so good when it's mulling! We make a big pot and take it outside with us on Halloween while we're handing out candy. Any leftover cider heats up wonderfully.

1 gal. apple cider or apple juice
1/2 to 3/4 c. brown sugar,
  packed
1 whole orange, unpeeled
15 to 20 whole cloves
2 to 3 4-inch cinnamon sticks

Pour cider into a slow cooker. Stir in desired amount of brown sugar. Stud orange with cloves; add to cider along with cinnamon sticks. Cover and cook on low setting for 2 to 3 hours, but do not boil. May be kept at serving temperature in slow cooker for several hours. Makes 16 servings.

Gather everyone for a fireside meal...so cozy on a chilly day! Cook hot dogs on long forks or use pie irons to make pocket pies. You can even roast foil-wrapped potatoes in the coals. Let the kids make s'mores for a sweet ending.

Index

Index

Index

Have a taste for more?

We created our official Circle of Friends so we could
fill everyone in on the latest scoop at once.
Visit us online to join in the fun and discover free
recipes, exclusive giveaways and much more!

www.gooseberrypatch.com

Join
Our Circle of
Friends

Find
Gooseberry
Patch
in Your
Neighborhood

Find us on
Facebook

You Tube

Follow us on
twitter

Read Our
Blog

Call us toll-free at 1·800·854·6673

U.S. to Canadian recipe equivalents

Volume Measurements

1/4 teaspoon	1 mL
1/2 teaspoon	2 mL
1 teaspoon	5 mL
1 tablespoon = 3 teaspoons	15 mL
2 tablespoons = 1 fluid ounce	30 mL
1/4 cup	60 mL
1/3 cup	75 mL
1/2 cup = 4 fluid ounces	125 mL
1 cup = 8 fluid ounces	250 mL
2 cups = 1 pint =16 fluid ounces	500 mL
4 cups = 1 quart	1 L

Weights

1 ounce	30 g
4 ounces	120 g
8 ounces	225 g
16 ounces = 1 pound	450 g

Oven Temperatures

300° F	150° C
325° F	160° C
350° F	180° C
375° F	190° C
400° F	200° C
450° F	230° C

Baking Pan Sizes

Square

8x8x2 inches	2 L = 20x20x5 cm
9x9x2 inches	2.5 L = 23x23x5 cm

Rectangular

13x9x2 inches	3.5 L = 33x23x5 cm

Loaf

9x5x3 inches	2 L = 23x13x7 cm

Round

8x1-1/2 inches	1.2 L = 20x4 cm
9x1-1/2 inches	1.5 L = 23x4 cm